Extraction of an Exhaustible Resource under Uncertainty

Author's address:

Prof. Dr. Michael Hoel
Institute of Economics
University of Oslo
Box 1095 Blindern, Oslo 3
Norway

Extraction of an Exhaustible Resource under Uncertainty

by

Michael Hoel
University of Oslo
Institute of Economics

Verlag Anton Hain
Meisenheim GmbH
Königstein/Ts.

Oelgeschlager, Gunn & Hain
Publishers, Inc.
Cambridge, Massachusetts

International Standard Book Number: 0-89946-029-1

Library of Congress Catalog Card Number: 79-92374

CIP-Kurztitelaufnahme der Deutschen Bibliothek

Hoel, Michael:
Extraction of an exhaustible resource under uncertainty / by Michael Hoel. – Königstein/Ts. : Hain; Cambridge, Mass. : Oelgeschlager, Gunn and Hain, 1980.
(Mathematical systems in economics ; 51)
ISBN 3–445–12012–9

Reproduktion, Druck und Bindung: Friedrich Pustet, Regensburg
Printed in West Germany
ISBN 3-445-12012-9

SUMMARY

The essay treats the extraction of a non-renewable scarce natural resource which has a non-exhaustible substitute, produced with a "backstop technology". Two types of uncertainty are considered in a two-period model, namely uncertainty with respect to whether or not a backstop technology will become available in the second period and uncertainty with respect to the true size of the stock of exhaustible resources. Extraction paths are derived for the social optimum as well as for the three market structures (i) full competition, (ii) a monopoly controlling the natural resource and the substitute, and (iii) a monopoly controlling the natural resource and competitive firms supplying the substitute.

Comparisons are made between the various market structures and the social optimum in the presence of uncertainty. Furthermore, the essay gives comparisons between the different solutions which follow from alternative assumptions about the degree of risk aversion. In particular, the case of risk neutrality is compared with the case of risk aversion.

The introduction of uncertainty changes the extraction paths in different ways for the different market structures. The same is true for comparisons between the case of risk neutrality and the case of risk version. A consequence of this is that the relationships between the various market structures and the social optimum may be different under uncertainty than they are under certainty. In particular, it is shown that uncertainty with respect to whether or not a backstop technology will become available may make the initial resource extraction under the two market structures with a competitively supplied substitute higher than what is socially optimal, even for demand functions making this impossible in the case of certainty.

CONTENTS

	Page
1. Introduction	1
1.1. Introduction	1
1.2. How uncertainty will enter problems of resource extraction	1
1.3. The meaning of an optimal strategy	11
1.4. Further simplifying assumptions	18
1.5. An outline of the study	21
2. Socially optimal resource extraction with an uncertain backstop technology	23
2.1. Introduction	23
2.2. The general case	24
2.3. Linear demand function	27
2.4. Log-linear demand function	30
2.5. Summary of chapter 2	32
3. Perfect competition with an uncertain backstop technology ..	33
3.1. General considerations	33
3.2. The general case	35
3.3. Linear and log-linear demand functions	39
3.4. Summary of chapter 3	42
4. Full monopoly with an uncertain backstop technology	44
4.1. The general case	44
4.2. Linear demand function	51
4.3. Log-linear demand function	54
4.4. Summary of chapter 4	57
5. Monopoly of the resource with an uncertain backstop technology	58
5.1. The general case	58
5.2. Linear demand function	64
5.3. Log-linear demand function	66
5.4. Summary of chapter 5	68
6. Socially optimal and competitive resource extraction with an uncertain resource stock	70
6.1. Introduction	70
6.2. Socially optimal resource extraction	72

Page

6.3. The competitive solution 75
6.4. Linear and log-linear demand functions 77
6.5. Summary of chapter 6 78
7. Full monopoly with an uncertain resource stock 79
7.1. The general case 79
7.2. Linear demand function 88
7.3. Log-linear demand function 91
7.4. Summary of chapter 7 95
8. Monopoly of the resource with an uncertain resource stock ... 97
8.1. The general case 97
8.2. Linear demand function 107
8.3. Log-linear demand function 110
8.4. Summary of chapter 8 113
9. Concluding comments 115
9.1. Summary of some important results 115
9.2. Optimal resource extraction and market economies 117
Appendix 121
References 126

CHAPTER 1.
INTRODUCTION

1.1. Introduction.

The economics of natural resources has received increasing attention lately. Until recently, most contributions in this field have disregarded all types of uncertainty connected with resource extraction. In the last few years, however, several papers have appeared which analyze various types of uncertainty in the context of exhaustible resource extraction. These contributions will be referred to later, especially in section 1.2.

The present study treats optimal resource extraction and resource extraction under some alternative market structures, taking the possibility of a substitute for the resource into explicit consideration. While some of my earlier work (Hoel, 1978 a,b) has treated similar problems in the case of certainty, the present work analyzes various effects of uncertainty.

The next section gives a brief outline of the problems which will be treated. In particular, a discussion is given of how uncertainty may enter the analysis.

1.2. How uncertainty will enter problems of resource extraction.

Like in Hoel (1978 a,b), we shall assume that we have some depletable natural resource which has a perfect substitute in all uses. At the initial time point, $t = 0$, there is a fixed deposit S_o of the natural resource. The resource can be extracted at a unit cost c_1 which is independent of current and accumulated resource extraction. However, the accumulated extraction (after $t = 0$) cannot exceed the limit S_0. The unit cost of producing the substitute, c_2, is assumed to be higher than c_1. On the other hand, there is no limit on the accumulated production of this substitute. Nordhaus (1973) has called the technology permitting such production of a substitute for the resource a "backstop technology".

Calling the rate of resource extraction x_1 and the rate of substitute production x_2, we assume that there exists a demand function

$$x_1 + x_2 = h(p)$$

or

$$p = h^{-1}(x_1+x_2), \tag{1.1}$$

where p is the common price of the resource and the substitute.

A more thorough discussion of the assumptions made above are given in Hoel (1978a, chapters 1 and 10). The latter study gives an analysis of the time development of $x_1(t)$, $x_2(t)$ and $p(t)$, under various market structures. In all cases the resource extractors and substitute producers have an exogeneously given discount factor r, and the whole analysis assumes full certainty about everything entering the decision-makers' optimization problems.

Uncertainty can enter the problems mentioned above in several ways. There may be uncertainty about the unit costs c_1 and c_2, and competitive firms may face an uncertain price development. A monopolist may face an uncertain demand function, and if a social welfare function is defined, it may include the preference structures of the consumers, which there may be uncertainty connected with. Uncertainty of the types just mentioned are not specific to the economics of resource extraction, and have been treated by several economists more generally (see for instance Leland (1972) and Sandmo (1971)). In the context of resource extraction, uncertainty with respect to the cost of producing a substitute has been treated by Hanson (1977) and Hoel (1978c). Lewis (1977) and Weinstein and Zeckhauser (1975, pp. 381-386) have treated the case where the future demand of an exhaustible demand is uncertain.

There are at least two ways uncertainty can enter our problem which are specific to the problems of resource extraction. The most obvious way is that the quantity of the initial resource deposit, which limits the accumulated resource extraction, is not known with certainty. This clearly gives a more realistic description of the real world than assuming S_o known with certainty: Of all mineral and fossil resources in the world, probably none have reserves which are known with full certainty or even near certainty.

In Hoel (1978a,b) it is assumed that the backstop technology is known at the initial time point of the analysis. However, for some resources there does not exist any backstop technology at the present time, although scientists and engineers expect a backstop technology making substitute production possible sometime in the future. For instance, energy based on nuclear fusion has not yet passed the threshold of scientific feasibility, although many scientists believe that fusion energy will be a possible substitute for energy based on fossil and uranium resources sometime in the future. In all cases where a backstop technology is not yet feasible, it seems realistic to assume that the date of availability of such a technology is not known with certainty.

The present study treats the two types of uncertainty mentioned above. Some literature analyzes these types of uncertainty. Manne (1974) has analyzed a problem where the date of availability of a safe breeder reactor is uncertain. A more general analysis, which is more similar to the present study, has been given by Dasgupta and Heal (1974, pp. 18-25). However, both of these studies only analyze developments which in some sense are defined as socially optimal. Recently, Dasgupta and Stiglitz (1976) have treated similar market structures as those in Hoel (1978a), allowing for uncertainty with respect to the date of availability of a backstop technology. The present study has a lot in common with the work of Dasgupta and Stiglitz. An important difference is that Dasgupta and Stiglitz disregard risk aversion, which will be treated in the present study. Furthermore, most of the results of Dasgupta and Stiglitz are only derived for a specific demand function. In the present study a more general demand function is used. On the other hand, a rather restrictive assumption, which is not used by Dasgupta and Stiglitz, will be introduced in section 1.4.

Uncertainty about the magnitude of the initial resource stock has been treated in the context of a specific example by Massé (1962, pp.358-373). The example analyzed there concerns exploiting an oil field, where the purpose is to find the optimal investment pattern when the oil reserves are not known with certainty. More general treatments of uncertainty regarding the true size of the resource stock have been given by Cropper (1976), Gilbert (1979) Heal (1975), Kemp (1976, chapter 23) and Loury (1976). However, none of these studies analyze other market structures when this type of uncertainty exists. The present study analyzes this type of uncertainty for several market structures, taking the possibility of risk aversion and the existence of a backstop technology into account.

A third type of uncertainty concerns the outcome of exploration activities. If the level of exploration activity is treated as exogeneously given, uncertainty with respect to what increases in the resource stock the exploration will give is in principle very similar to uncertainty with regard to the true size of the initial resource stock. However, this similarity will no longer hold when exploration activity is considered as a variable in the analysis. Explicit treatment of exploration under uncertainty has been given by Gilbert(1976,1977 and 1979) and Solow (1977). The present study does not consider exploration activity as a variable in the analysis.

To get an understanding of the problems which arise when there is uncertainty about the quantity of the resource deposit or the date of availability of the backstop technology, we shall consider the latter type of uncertainty in some detail. However, the considerations given below also apply to uncertainty about S_o.

Look at a decision-maker in control of both the resource extraction $x_1(t)$ and the substitute production $x_2(t)$, and who has an objective function depending on the devopment of $x_1(t)$ and $x_2(t)$ from the initial time point $(t=0)$ till some given planning horizon (finite or infinite). This decision-maker could be a central planning agency or a reasource and substitute monopolist (cf. Hoel, 1978a, chapter 3). Let us first look at the case where the decision-maker has full certainty about everything concerning his decision problem, including the date of availability of the backstop technology, which we shall denote by θ. In this case maximization of the objective function taking all constraints into account (especially $x_2(t) = 0$ for $t<\theta$) will give the optimal decision for the future development of $x_1(t)$ and $x_2(t)$. Even if the decision at $t = 0$ is not binding, it will never be optimal for the decision-maker to change his plan unless his objective function changes[1].

Let us now turn to the case where θ is not known with certainty, but where the decision-maker has an opinion about the probabilities of various values of θ. Such an opinion can be formalized by assuming that there exists a subjective probability density function $\xi_o(\theta)$ at the initial time point. This density function may for instance have a form like in figure 1.1a or 1.1b, but other forms are of course also conceivable. If we call the

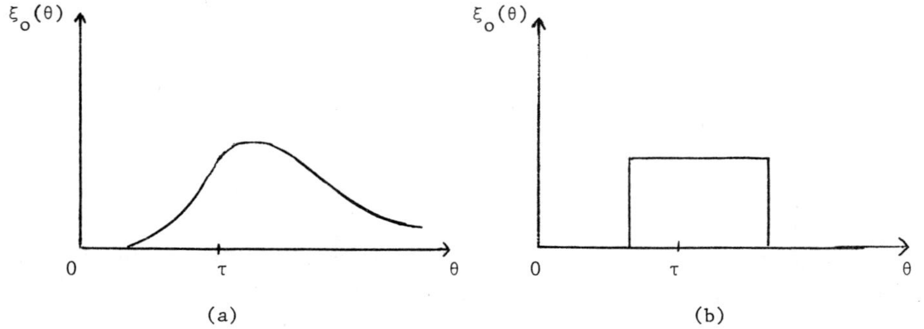

Figure 1.1

probability of a backstop technology *never* becoming feasible Ω_o, we must have

$$(1.2) \qquad \Omega_o = 1 - \int_o^\infty \xi_o(\theta)d\theta \geqq 0.$$

---

1) It is not quite precise what is meant by an unchanged objective function. Look at the case where time is discret, $x(t)$ is the value in period t of the vector of variables entering the objective function, and T is the planning horizon. With an unchanged objective function we mean that if the objective function at $t=0$ is $\Phi(x(1),x(2),\ldots,x(T))$, then the objective function function at $t = \tau$ may be written as $\Phi(\bar{x}(1),\ldots,\bar{x}(\tau),x(\tau+1),\ldots,x(T))$ where $\bar{x}(1),\ldots,\bar{x}(\tau)$ are given in period τ. Problems occuring when the objective function does not have this property have been treated by Strotz (1955) and Pollak (1968).

When θ is unknown, the decision-maker can obviously not make any decision about the future development of $x_2(t)$ at $t = 0$. Or more precisely, the only possible decision about $x_2(t)$ which the decision maker feels certain he will be able to carry through is

$$(1.3) \qquad x_2(t) = 0 \text{ for all } t \text{ such that } \int_0^t \xi_0(\theta)d\theta < 1.$$

In particular, if $\Omega_0 > 0$ or if $\xi_0(\Theta) > 0$ no matter how large θ is, $x_2(t)=0$ for all t is the only possible binding decision which can be made at t=0.

From what we have said above it is clear that the decision-maker imposes a strong restriction on his possible actions if he only considers decisions which are binding from t=0. To avoid such a restriction, he can make a *strategy* at t=0 instead of a binding decision. The consept of strategy was first introduced by von Neuman and Morgenstern (1947), and consists of rules telling the decision-maker how he should respond to information gathered up to each point of time in the future. Or in the words of von Neuman and Morgenstern (1947, p. 79), "... the strategy is supposed to specify each individual decision as a function of the exact bundle of information available at the moment the decision must be made". The decision-maker's problem is now not to make a final decision about the development of $x_1(t)$ and $x_2(t)$, but to choose the strategy which in some sense is the best, of all possible strategies. To formalize, call the information available at each future time point I_t. A strategy for how to choose $x_1(t)$ and $x_2(t)$ is then given by two functions $R_1(\cdot)$ and $R_2(\cdot)$:

$$(1.4) \qquad \begin{cases} x_1(t) = R_1(I_t), \\ \\ x_2(t) = R_2(I_t). \end{cases}$$

At any future time point I_t will be given, and (1.4) will determine $x_1(t)$ and $x_2(t)$. The decision-maker's problem is to find functions $\hat{R}_1(\cdot)$ and $\hat{R}_2(\cdot)$ which in some sense are at least as good as all other possible choices of $R_1(\cdot)$ and $R_2(\cdot)$. In the next section we shall explain in some more detail what we shall mean by an optimal strategy. But first we shall use the rest of this section to point out what type of information the decision-maker can receive in the future.

The most obvious information the decision-maker will have at some future time point, say τ, is whether the backstop technology is feasible or not at τ. If $\xi_o(\theta) > 0$ for some $\theta < \tau$, like in figure 1.1, this means that the decision-maker will have information at τ which he did not have initially (i.e. when $t = 0$). If the backstop technology is feasible at τ, there will be no more uncertainty after τ. On the other hand, there will be uncertainty also after τ if the backstop technology has not yet become feasible at τ. In this case it seems reasonable to assume that the decision-maker will have some opinion about the probability of various values of θ at the time point τ, just like he had when $t = 0$. This opinion will of course depend on all information received up till τ. In addition to the information that the backstop technology is not feasible at τ, the decision-maker may have information about scientific and technical developments after $t = 0$. Like before, the decision-maker's opinion about various values of θ can be formalized by assuming that there exists a subjective probability density function $\xi_\tau(\theta, I_\tau)$ at τ. Like before we can define

(1.5) $$\Omega_\tau = 1 - \int_\tau^\infty \xi_\tau(\theta, I_\tau) d\theta$$

as the probability of a backstop technology never becoming feasible, *given* that it has not become feasible at τ

Let us first assume that the decision-maker does not receive any new information after $t = 0$ except whether or not a backstop technology has become feasible. In this simple case it seems reasonable that the *conditional* probability of the backstop technology becoming available at t, given that it has not become available before t, is unchanged as time proceeds from 0 to t. At t = 0, these conditional probabilities are defined by

$$(1.6) \qquad \tilde{\xi}_o(\theta) = \xi_o(\theta)[1 - \int_o^\theta \xi_o(s)ds]^{-1},$$

while the same conditional probabilities at τ are defined by

$$(1.7) \qquad \tilde{\xi}_\tau(\theta,I_\tau) = \xi_\tau(\theta,I_\tau)[1 - \int_\tau^\theta \xi_\tau(s,I_\tau)ds]^{-1}.$$

Now it is easy to show that $\tilde{\xi}_\tau(\theta,I_\tau) = \tilde{\xi}_o(\theta)$ for all τ if

$$(1.8) \qquad \xi_\tau(\theta,I_\tau) = \xi_o(\theta)[1 - \int_o^\tau \xi_o(s)ds]^{-1},$$

which also implies that

$$(1.9) \qquad \Omega_\tau = \Omega_o[1 - \int_o^\tau \xi_o(s)ds]^{-1}.$$

To illustrate, this means that once we have reached τ in figure 1.1, the new density function follows from the old one by simply multiplying the old values with a constant equal to the inverse of one minus the area under the old function to the left of τ. In figure 1.2 the broken line is the original density function, while the fully drawn line represents the decision-makers' density function when τ is reached without the backstop technology having become available:

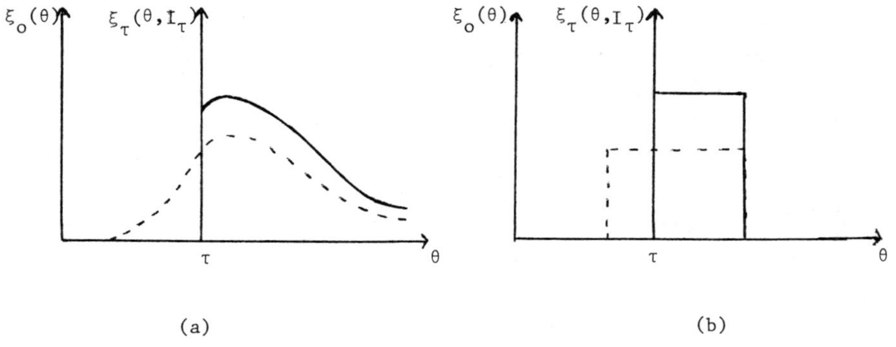

Figure 1.2

The simple assumption about the connection between $\xi_o(\theta)$ and $\xi_\tau(\theta, I_\tau)$ just treated in a sense means that the decision-maker's opinion about how probable various dates of availability are stays unchanged. It is an assumption of this kind which has been used in several of the studies referred to in section 1.2. This assumption may seem relatively reasonable, but once we allow for other types of information (for instance scientific and technical), things might not be so simple. In this case it seems reasonable to expect the probability density function to change in a more fundamental way than what we have just discussed. Such a more fundamental change in the density function is perhaps especially important in the case where it is the magnitude of the resource deposit which is not known with certainty. In this case it seems reasonable to expect new information about this magnitude to follow as a joint product of exploiting the resource.

We mentioned earlier that $x_1(t)$ and $x_2(t)$ are determined by a strategy given by functions like in (1.4). These functions $R_1(\cdot)$ and $R_2(\cdot)$ are chosen at t = 0, and seen from this time point the future information is obviously not known with certainty, so that the results $x_1(t)$ and $x_2(t)$ also are uncertain. To choose the best possible functions $\hat{R}_1(\cdot)$ and $\hat{R}_2(\cdot)$, the decision-maker must therefore not only have an opinion about the density functions $\xi_o(\theta)$ and $\xi_\tau(\theta, I_\tau)$ for all $\tau > 0$, but he must also have some opinion about what kind of future information he will get. For instance, a decision-maker regarding the possibilities of future fusion energy may in the year 1980 believe that fusion energy will become available in the period 2000 to 2100 with a probability of π, with all dates in this period having equal probability, and that the probability of fusion energy *never* becoming available is $1 - \pi$. In addition to such a probability function, the decision-maker must have some opinion about what kind of new information he will receive conserning the possibilities of fusion energy. He may know - or expect with a large probability - that he will receive scientific information before the year 2000 which will make him able to know *with certainty* whether or not fusion energy ever will become feasible, and perhaps also more precisely *when* it will become available, if ever. One would generally expect his choice of strategy to be different in this case than in a case where he expects to receive *no* additional information in the future, except of course whether or not fusion energy actually has become feasible at these future time points.

It is clear that an analysis taking all the points mentioned above into account would become very complicated, probably unmanagable. These difficulties will, however, be avoided in the present study, thanks to the simplifying assumptions we shall introduce in section 1.4.

1.3. The meaning of an optimal strategy.

In the preceding section we showed that a decision-maker would not make a final decision about how to extract a natural resource when there was uncertainty, but would choose a strategy telling him how to react upon future information. We shall now explain what we mean by an optimal strategy. To do this, it is convenient to start by stating what objective function the decision-makers in our analysis would maximize in the case of certainty.

Let us start by explaining what we shall mean by a social optimum. We shall assume that in addition to resource extraction, and possibly substitute production, only one aggregate good is produced in the economy. This good is produced by producable real capital, $K(t)$, our resource and/or substitute, $x(t) = x_1(t) + x_2(t)$, and primary factors whose time development is considered exogeneous. The aggregate good can be used as a final good for consumption, $y(t)$, and investment in real capital, $\dot{K}(t)$, and as an intermediate good for resource extraction, $c_1x_1(t)$, or production of the substitute (if technically feasible), $c_2x_2(t)$. In other words c_1 and c_2 are the unit costs, in terms of the aggregate good, of resource extraction and substitute production, respectively. Calling our production function Φ we therefore have

$$(1.10) \qquad y(t) + \dot{K}(t) + c_1x_1(t) + c_2x_2(t) = \Phi(K(t), x_1(t) + x_2(t), t).$$

We shall assume that the society's welfare level is given by some function of the time development of consumption from 0 till T,[1] which we denote by $\Psi(\cdot)$. Calling society's welfare level W, we therefore have

$$(1.11) \qquad W = \Psi(y(\cdot)).$$

1) This type of function is often called a functional.

The function Ψ need not be specified, we shall only assume that it has the property that increased consumption in some period has a positive effect on the welfare level, cet.par. Or more precisely, we assume that $\Psi(y(\cdot)+\gamma(\cdot)) > \Psi(y(\cdot))$ for all $y(\cdot)$ and $\gamma(\cdot)$ such that $\gamma(t) \geqq 0$ for all $t \in [0,T]$ and $\gamma(t)>0$ for $t \in [\tau',\tau'']$ where τ' and τ'' are arbitrary except that $0 \leqq \tau' < \tau'' \leqq T$.

A social optimum is defined as time developments $(\hat{K}(\cdot),\hat{x}_1(\cdot),\hat{x}_2(\cdot))$ such that (1.11) is maximized subject to (1.10) and whatever constraints one has on $K(\cdot)$, $x_1(\cdot)$ and $x_2(\cdot)$. We shall assume that the only constraints we have on $K(t)$ are given by

$$(1.12) \qquad K(0) = K_o,\ K(T) \geqq K_T,$$

where K_o and K_T are non-negative. The constraints on $x_1(\cdot)$ and $x_2(\cdot)$ are

$$(1.13) \qquad x_i(\cdot) \in X_i \qquad\qquad i = 1,2,$$

where X_1 and X_2 are two given sets of time paths, given in detail in the appendix.

The solution of the problem above of course depends on the exact specification of ψ. However, whatever specification ψ has, it can be shown (see the appendix) that the optimal solution $(\hat{K}(\cdot),\hat{x}_1(\cdot),\hat{x}_2(\cdot))$ must satisfy the following inequality; which is an efficiency condition of the type discussed by Dorfman, Samuelson and Solow (1958, chapter 12):

$$(1.14) \qquad J(\hat{x}_1(\cdot),\hat{x}_2(\cdot)) \geqq J(x_1(\cdot),x_2(\cdot)) \text{ for all } x_1(\cdot) \in X_1 \text{ and } x_2(\cdot) \in X_2,$$

where

$$(1.15) \qquad J(x_1(\cdot),x_2(\cdot)) = \int_0^T e^{-\int_0^t r(\tau)d\tau} [\Phi(\hat{K}(t),x_1(t)+x_2(t),t)-c_1x_1(t)-c_2x_2(t)]dt$$

and

$$(1.16) \qquad r(\tau) = \frac{\partial\Phi(\hat{K}(t),\hat{x}_1(t) + \hat{x}_2(t),t)}{\partial K}.$$

The inequality above only describes a connection between $\hat{K}(\cdot)$ on the one hand and $\hat{x}_1(\cdot)$ and $\hat{x}_2(\cdot)$ on the other hand. The actual solution $(\hat{K}(\cdot), \hat{x}_1(\cdot),\hat{x}_2(\cdot))$ will of course depend on Ψ. However, we shall not be concerned with the optimal development of the capital stock in the present study. We shall therefore regard $\hat{K}(\cdot)$ as given, which means that $J(x_1(\cdot), x_2(\cdot))$ from (1.15) may be used as our objective function when studying what resource extraction and substitute production is socially optimal.

The discount factor r(t) given by (1.16) stands for the rate of return on capital, and will generally depend on the optimal development of $x_1(t) + x_2(t)$. However, like in Hoel (1978a,b) and several other studies of resource extraction, we shall assume that r(t) may be considered as independent of $\hat{x}_1(t) + \hat{x}_2(t)$. Furthermore, we shall simplify our notation by assuming that r(t) is constant.

In the beginning of section 1.2 we made the simplifying assumption that the demand for $x_1 + x_2$ only depended on the price p (in terms of the aggregate good). However, if the produsers of the aggregate good are profit maximizing price takers, their demand is given by

$$(1.17) \qquad \frac{\partial\Phi(\hat{K}(t),x_1(t) + x_2(t),t)}{\partial(x_1(t) + x_2(t))} = p(t).$$

Normally, p will therefore depend on t as well as on $x_1 + x_2$, so that the demand function may not be written like we did in (1.1). Using self-explaining notation for the second order derivatives and $x = x_1 + x_2$, it is clear that the demand function (1.1) corresponds to (1.17) if and only if

$$(1.18) \qquad \Phi_{xK} \frac{d\hat{K}(t)}{dt} + \Phi_{xt} = 0 \text{ for all x and t, when } K(t) = \hat{K}(t).$$

For r(t) to be independent of x we obviously must have $\Phi_{xK} = 0$, cf. (1.16). Together with (1.18) this implies $\Phi_{xt} = \Phi_{xK} = 0$, which means that the production function must have the following form:

$$(1.19) \qquad \Phi(K,x,t) = \alpha(K,t) + \phi(x).$$

This is a rather restrictive production function. In particular, it excludes the possibility of the natural resource being essential, in the sense that $\Phi(K,o,t) = 0$ for all K (assuming $\alpha_K(K,t) > 0$). However, it is not necessary for our purpose that (1.19) holds for all (K,x,t), it need only hold for $K = \hat{K}(t)$ and over the range of x which is relevant in our analysis. If the natural resource studied does not have a too dominant role in the economy, (1.19) therefore may be a reasonably good approximation of the production function.

With the necessary qualification if (1.19) only holds over a certain range of x, the term $\phi(x)$ represents the contribution to the gross production of the aggregate good which follows from using the amount x of the resource and/or the substitute. This interpretation of course requires that the functions $\alpha(K,t)$ and $\phi(x)$ have been constructed so that $\phi(0) = 0$.

When (1.19) holds, it follows from (1.17) that our demand function is given by

$$(1.20) \qquad p = h^{-1}(x) = \phi'(x).$$

Furthermore, from (1.16) and (1.19) we see that

$$(1.21) \qquad r(t) = \frac{\delta\alpha(\hat{K}(t),t)}{\delta K},$$

i.e. r(t) is exogeneous when $\hat{K}(t)$ is considered exogeneous.

Using (1.19) and assuming for notational convenience that the discount factor r(t) is constant, we may rewrite the objective function (1.15) as

$$(1.22) \qquad J = Z + Z^{o},$$

where

$$(1.23) \qquad Z = \int_{0}^{T} e^{-rt}[\phi(x_1(t) + x_2(t)) - c_1x_1(t) - c_2x_2(t)]dt$$

and

$$Z^{o} = \int_{0}^{T} e^{-rt}\alpha(\hat{K}(t),t)dt.$$

Since Z^{o} is exogeneous in our analysis, maximizing J is the same as maximizing Z, we may therefore use (1.23) as the social objective function in the case of certainty. From what we have shown above, it is clear that (1.23) stands for the discounted value of the contribution to consumption plus investment which follows from resource extraction and substitute production. This objective function is quite similar to the ones used for instance by Hotelling (1931) and Weinstein and Zeckhauser (1974 and 1975).

They use discounted consumers surplus minus costs of extraction/production, which is precisely what (1.23) stands for, except that the "consumers" here are the producers using the natural resource (and/or the produced substitute) as an input in their production of the aggregate good.

Let us now turn to the case where uncertainty enters our problem. In the preceding section we argued that $x_1(t)$ and $x_2(t)$ would be determined by a stategy like in (1.4). But this means that at $t = 0$, the future devepment of $x_1(t)$ and $x_2(t)$ will be uncertain whatever decision rules $R_1(\cdot)$ and $R_2(\cdot)$ are chosen. Therefore the value of J, given by (1.15), will also be some stocastic variable for any given strategy.[1] It therefore has no meaning to try to choose $R_1(\cdot)$ and $R_2(\cdot)$ so that J is maximized. The usual procedure in such cases is to assume that there exists a von Neuman - Morgenstern utility function U(J). Such a function has the property that maximization of EU(J) (i.e. the expected value of U(J)) will give us the distribution of possible values of J which the decision-maker ranks highest of all possible distributions.[2] From (1.22) we see that $EU(J) = EU(Z + Z^o)$, so that if Z is small compared with Z^o and $U''(Z^o)$ is not too large, we can use the following approximation:

$$(1.24) \qquad EU(Z + Z^o) \approx E[U(Z^o) + U'(Z^o)Z] = U(Z^o) + U'(Z^o)EZ$$

This means that maximization of EZ, where Z is given by (1.23), will give us the same result as maximization of EU(J).[3] We shall therefore assume that the society's objective is to maximize the expected value

1) In the case of uncertainty, it is not obvious that J should be taken as our starting point: We have seen that maximization of W given by (1.11) implied that J was maximized in the case of certainty. But it is not obvious that a similar relationship holds in the case of uncertainty. And even if such a relationship does hold, the optimal $\hat{K}(t)$, and therefore also the function J, will in general depend on whether or not there is uncertainty. However, we shall disregard these problems, and use J given by (1.15) as our starting point. This can probably be justified if we assume that $\phi(x(t))$ is small compared with $\alpha(\hat{K}(t),t)$, so that the uncertain part of J is small compared with J.

2) See for instance Arrow (1965).

3) This result of course only holds exactly when $U''(J) = 0$ for $J \in [Z^o, Z^o+Z]$, i.e. when we have risk neutrality.

of Z given by (1.23) in the case of uncertainty. The same assumption is made in most of the studies referred to in section 1.2. However, we shall also mention how the social optimum will be affected if we instead of maximizing EZ maximize the expected value of some concave function of Z.

As already mentioned, this study is not only concerned with analyzing the socially optimal development of $x_1(t)$ and $x_2(t)$ under uncertainty. We shall also treat several market structures, and compare these with the social optimum. Under all market structures we shall assume that the resource extracting firms are interested in making their discounted profits, V, as high as possible. Uncertainty will be taken care of by assuming that the resource extractors have a von Neuman-Morgenstern utility function U(V). In the case of the social optimum, Z was only a small part of J, so that we could maximize EZ even if $U''(J) \neq 0$, i.e. even if society is not risk neutral with respect to J. For the individual firms we shall assume that they are not involved in other income earning activities, so that V consists only of discounted profits from resource extraction[1]. The function U therefore must be applied directly on V, so that we cannot disregard the cases where $U''(V) \neq 0$. In particular, we shall study the case where $U''(V) < 0$, i.e. the firms have risk aversion.

---

1) In one of our market structures profits from any substitute production will also enter V.

1.4. Further simplifying assumptions.

We shall now introduce some further simplifications in order to make the analysis easier to handle and follow.

The analysis in Hoel (1978a,b) regarded time as continuous. In the case of uncertainty, it is somewhat simpler to treat time as a discrete variable, which we therefore shall do in the present study. Instead of looking at t increasing continuously over the interval [0,T], we therefore assume that we have T periods (1,2,...,T), and that t stands for the current period.

The most drastic simplification we shall use is that we shall only consider two periods, i.e. T = 2. This of course makes our analysis much simpler than if T > 2, but it also reduces the importance of the conclusions, as one cannot know a priori if they generalize to T > 2. In a sense, however, all conclusions can generalize to the case where T > 2: As T = 2 is a special case of a multi-period analysis, any conclusion about for instance the sign of a variable (or difference between variables) is a *possible* outcome of the more general case with $T \geqq 2$. If one knows that in the case of certainty this outcome *never* will occur in the general case of $T \geqq 0$, this is an important conclusion concerning the difference between cases with and without uncertainty. For instance, in Hoel (1978a) it was shown that, with the assumptions made there, a monopolist would *always* extract less of the resource initially than the resource extraction under competitive conditions. Furthermore, it is easy to show that with a social objective function similar to (1.23), the resource extraction under competitive conditions is socially optimal (see for instance Dasgupta and Stiglitz (1976) and Sweeney (1977)). If, using the same assuptions except for introducing uncertainty, one can find that a monopolist possibly extracts *more* of the resource initially than what is socially optimal, this gives us interesting information even when derived from a two-period analysis.

Throughout our analysis, we shall assume that no backstop technology exists in period 1. The two types of uncertainty we shall study are that (i) there is uncertainty concerning the possibilities of a backstop technology becoming feasible in period 2, and (ii) the resource deposit S_0 is not known with certainty. In both cases we shall assume that the uncertainty occurs in the beginning of period 1, when decisions for period 1 must be made. Before decisions for period 2 are made, the decision-makers know with certainty whether or not a backstop technology is feasible and how much there is left of the resource deposit. We shall return to the more exact specification of how uncertainty is treated in the relevant chapters.

To simplify the mathematical sides of our analysis, we shall assume that U(V) and $\phi(x)$, which are the two functions entering the analysis, both are continuous and differentiable as many times as we require. Furthermore, we shall assume that

$$(1.25) \qquad U'(V) > 0 \quad , \quad U''(V) \leqq 0 \qquad \text{for all } V \geqq 0$$

and

$$(1.26) \qquad \phi'(x) > 0, \quad \phi''(x) < 0, \quad 2\phi''(x+x^*) + x\phi'''(x+x^*) \leqq 0 \text{ for all } x,x^* \geqq 0.$$

In other words, U(V) is a strictly increasing concave function while $\phi(x)$ is strictly increasing and strictly concave. The last inequality in (1.26) states that the function $x\phi'(x+x^*)$, which will enter the optimization problem of a monopolist (cf. 1.20), is concave in x.

For our problem of resource extraction to be of any interest, we must assume that the resource is so scarce that it will be used up during the two periods under all optimization problems considered. The following condition is sufficient for this to be the case:

$$(1.27) \qquad \phi'(\frac{S_o}{2}) + \frac{S_o}{2}\phi''(\frac{S_o}{2}) > c_1,$$ [1)]

where c_1 is the unit cost of resource extraction. This inequality implies that if there was no limit on the accumulated resource extraction, a monopolist would choose $x > S_o/2$ in both periods. In other words, the initial resource stock S_o is an effective constraint on the monopolist's

1) This and the next condition is based on a known S_o. In chapter 6 we shall specify how these conditions are changed in the case of uncertainty with respect to S_o.

choice of extraction. Together with (1.26) it is clear that (1.27) implies

$$(1.27') \qquad \phi'(\frac{S_o}{2}) > c_1,$$

so that the extraction in the competitive and socially optimal solution is effectively constrained by S_o.

Although the decision-maker does not know whether or not a backstop technology will be feasible in period 2, we shall assume that the unit costs of substitute production, c_2, *if* such production becomes possible, is known with certainty already before the decisions for period 1 are made. It would of course be more reasonable to assume that c_2 is not known with certainty before one knows if substitute production will be possible. On the other hand, one may perhaps be more uncertain about if a backstop technology will become feasible than one is about the characteristics it will have, here given by c_2, if such a technology becomes feasible. Like Dasgupta and Heal (1974, p.19) and Dasgupta and Stiglitz (1976, p.5), we shall therefore disregard uncertainty about c_2.[1)]

To make some of our discussion simpler, we shall assume that

$$(1.28) \qquad \phi'(\frac{S_o}{2}) > c_2$$

This assumption means that the unit costs of substitute production are lower than what the resource price would be if the level of extraction was the same in both periods.

Finally, to simplify some of our expression, we shall disregard costs of resource extractions, i.e. we shall assume

---

1) If c_2 was uncertain in the beginning of period 1, a sufficiently wide range of possible values of c_2 would make it unnecessary to consider whether or not the backstop technology will become feasible. The reason for this is that if c_2 turns out to be sufficiently high, the backstop technology will not be used in period 2 in any case. In this case it is unimportant, from an economic point of view, whether or not such a technology is *technically* feasible. Hanson (1977) treats uncertainty in c_2 in a way which includes the possibility of the backstop technology not becoming econimically feasible.

(1.29) $c_1 = 0$.

Of all the simplifications above it is the assumption about T = 2 and c_2 known with certainty which are most important from an economic point of view. The assumption (1.27) is of course also important, without it our two-period analysis could degenerate into an uninteresting problem where the fixed supply of the natural resource was without importance. The rest of our simplifying assumptions are less important, and are only made to simplify the exposition.

The analysis of Dasgupta and Stiglitz (1976) is more general than the present one, as they treat time continuously and therefore do not limit themselves to a two-period analysis. On the other hands, the following analysis will treat several topics which Dasgupta and Stiglitz do not treat. Whenever possible our result will be compared with those of Dasgupta and Stiglitz.

1.5. An outline of the study.

The next four chapters concern uncertainty about whether or not substitute production will become possible in period 2. In these chapters the resource deposit S_0 is assumed to be known with certainty. We shall find the socially optimal solution, and compare this solution with three of the market structures studied in Hoel (1978a). These three are (i) perfect competition, (ii) full monopoly and (ii) monopolized resource extraction. The first market structure needs no comment. By full monopoly we mean that a single monopolist has control over all the resource extraction, and also the bakcstop technology if it becomes feasible. The reason for the same monopolist controlling both resource extraction and substitute production could be that most technical development leading to the backstop technology is carried out be the resource extracting monopolist, and that this monopolist can manage to prevent others from using the results of this technical development. The oil industry provides an example of resource extracting firms engaging in research for a backstop technologies: Several large oil companies are engaged in finding alternative energy sources.

The third market structure we shall study is the case where a monopolist has control over the resource extraction, but *not* over the backstop technology, if it becomes feasible. Such a structure can occur even if the resource extracting monopolist is engaged in technical development leading to the backstop technology, if the monopolist has no means to prevent others from using the results following from the technical development.

The solutions for the social optimum and the three market structures will first be derived without specifying the demand function $p = \phi'(x)$. However, some comparisons will be made using two specific demand function, namely linear and log-linear. A linear demand function is used to make comparisons with Hoel (1978a) easier, as such a demand function is used there. A log-linear demand function is used because it has the interesting property that when a backstop technology with certainty will *not* become feasible, the solutions of all three market structures as well as the social optimum are identical, as we shall see. This demand function is also used by Dasgupta and Stiglitz (1976) and Hoel (1978b).

The introduction of specific demand functions makes numerical examples possible. Such examples will be given, in order to give a feeling of the numerical importance of differences between the various market structures and of differences between degrees of uncertainty and of risk aversion.

Chapters 6 - 8 treat uncertainty of the magnitude of the resource deposit S_o. In these chapters it will be assumed that the backstop technology will be feasible with certainty in the second period. The social optimum will be compared with the same market structures as before, and the same specific demand functions will be used. A lot of the analysis in these chapters will necessarily be quite similar to the analysis in chapter 2 - 5. To avoid too much repitition, some of the discussion and interpretations in chapters 6 - 8 are therefore less detailed than in chapters 2 - 5. This is particularly true for the sections containing specific demand functions and numerical examples.

Chapter 9 concludes the study, giving a discussion and a comparison of the two types of uncertainty.

CHAPTER 2.

SOCIALLY OPTIMAL RESOURCE EXTRACTION WITH AN UNCERTAIN BACKSTOP TECHNOLOGY.

2.1. Introduction.

In this and the next three chapters S (the subscript o is omitted in the rest of the analysis for notational convenience) is assumed to be known with certainty. There is no backstop technology in period 1, while the probability of a backstop technology becoming available in period 2 is considered to be π in the beginning of period 1 by whatever decision-maker we are considering.[1] Before decisions for period 2 are made, the decision-maker knows whether or not substitute production is possible in this period. In the present chapter our decision-maker is a central planning agency with the objective function given by (1.23), while chapters 3-5 treat the cases where the decision-maker is a profit maximizing firm[2]. In the present two-period discrete time case the objective function (1.23) takes the form

$$(2.1) \qquad Z = \phi(x_1) + (1+r)^{-1}[\phi(S-x_1+x_2) - cx_2],$$

where the following notation is used in addition to the notational simplification $c_2 = c$ (since $c_1 = 0$):

x_1 = resource extraction in period 1,

$S-x_1$ = resource extraction in period 2,

x_2 = substitute production in period 2.

This notation can be used because of our assumption (1.27), which implies that all of the resource deposit will be used up during the two periods, at least as long as S is certain.

---

1) We shall disregard problems arising when π is considered different by different decision-makers.

2) In the competitive case there are of course several decision-makers.

2.2. The general case.

The social optimum can be found by using our notion of a strategy introduced in section 1.2 (pp. 6 - 7). Whatever value for x_1 one has chosen in the beginning of period 1, it is clear that in period 2 x_2 must be given by a rule of the following type:

$$(2.2)\qquad \begin{cases} x_2 = 0 \text{ if a backstop technology is not feasible,} \\ x_2 = \hat{x}_2(x_1) \text{ if a backstop technology is feasible.} \end{cases}$$

The function $\hat{x}_2(x_1)$ defines the value of x_2 which maximizes Z for whatever value of x_1 one has chosen. From (2.1) it is clear that $\hat{x}_2(x_1)$ must be given by

$$(2.3)\qquad \phi'(S - x_1 + \hat{x}_2(x_1)) = c \ .$$

Here we have disregarded the possibility of $\hat{x}_2(x_1)=0$, as this only would be optimal if $\phi'(S - x_1) \leqq c$. From (1.28) it is clear that this can only occur if $x_1 < S/2$, and as we soon shall see, the optmal value of x_1 will never be so small.

In the beginning of period 1 the decision-maker does not know whether $x_2 = 0$ or $x_2 = \hat{x}_2(x_1)$, because he does not yet know if the backstop technology will be feasible. The value of Z will therefore be uncertain for any given value of x_1. The choice of x_1 is therefore made by maximizing EZ, i.e. the expected value of Z(cf. section 1.3, pp. 16 - 17). Maximizing EZ is of course the same as maximizing (1+r)EZ, which is given by the following expression:

$$(2.4)\qquad (1+r)EZ = (1+r)\phi(x_1)+\pi[\phi(S - x_1+\hat{x}_2(x_1))-c\ \hat{x}_2(x_1)]+(1-\pi)\phi(S - x_1) \cdot$$

Now (1+r)EZ is concave in x_1, using (2.3) it is therefore clear that a necessary and sufficient condition for $\hat{x}_1$ to maximize (1+r)EZ is that

$$(2.5)\qquad \begin{cases} (1+r)\phi'(\hat{x}_1) = f(\hat{x}_1,\pi) \\ \text{or } \hat{x}_1 = 0 \text{ and } (1+r)\phi'(0) \leqq f(0,\pi) \\ \text{or } \hat{x}_1 = S \text{ and } (1+r)\phi'(S) \geqq f(S,\pi)\ , \end{cases}$$

where

$$(2.6)\qquad f(x_1,\pi) = \pi c + (1-\pi)\phi'(S-x_1).$$

The functions $(1+r)\phi'(x_1)$ and $f(x_1,\pi)$ are illustrated in figure 2.1. The fully drawn downward sloping curve is the graph of $(1+r)\phi'(x_1)$, which lies further to the right the higher is r. The increasing dotted curve

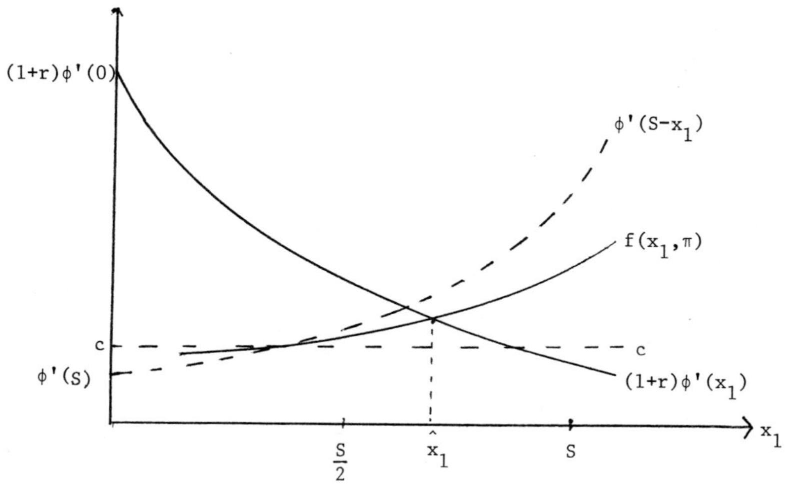

Figure 2.1.

is the graph of $\phi'(S-x_1)$, and is the mirror image of $\phi'(x_1)$ around a vertical axis going through $x_1 = S/2$. Because $r \geq 0$, the intersection of these two curves cannot be to the left of S/2. The horizontal dotted curve represents c, and lies below the intersection point of the two former curves, because $\phi'(S-x_1) \geq \phi'(S/2)$ for $x_1 \geq S/2$ and $\phi'(S/2) > c$ (cf. (1.28)).

The graph of $f(x_1,\pi)$ is simply a weighted average - with π and $1-\pi$ as weights - of c and $\phi'(S-x_1)$. This graph is given by the fully drawn increasing curve in figure 2.1. The intersection between this curve and $(1+r)\phi'(x_1)$ gives us $\partial(1+r)EZ/\partial x_1 = 0$, so that $\hat{x}_1$ in figure 2.1 is the socially optimal resource extraction in period 1.

From our reasoning above it is clear that a solution $x_1 = 0$ cannot be optimal. Actually, we must have $\hat{x}_1 > S/2$, except for the case where $r = \pi = 0$, when $\hat{x}_1 = S/2$. However, the corner solution $\hat{x}_1 = S$ is possible, and will occur if $(1+r)\phi'(S) \geq f(S,\pi)$, which is possible if r is sufficiently high or c and $1-\pi$ are sufficiently close to zero. Although $\hat{x}_1 = S$ is possible, this corner solution will not be explicitly taken into consideration in formulas, figures and conclusions in the rest of the present study. The only place where $\hat{x}_1 = S$ will be explicitly considered is when a numerical example gives this solution.

It is clear from figure 2.1 that the optimal resource extraction in period 1 ($=\hat{x}_1$) is higher the higher is the discount factor r and the probability of the backstop technology becoming feasible and higher the lower the cost of substitute production, if possible, is. Obviously, $\hat{x}_1$ is also higher the higher S is.

2.3. *Linear demand function.*

We now assume, like in Hoel (1978a), that our demand function is linear, i.e.

$$(2.7) \qquad p = a - bx,$$

where a and b are positive. Together with (1.20) this means that

$$(2.8) \qquad \phi'(x) = a - bx.$$

It is clear from (2.8) that $\phi(x)$ is an increasing function, like we have assumed (cf. (1.26)), only for $x < a/b$. To be able to use this linear demand function, we must therefore assume that a/b is so large that values of x higher than a/b are of no interest in our analysis. This will be true if $a/b > S$.

The function $\phi(x)$ giving us (2.8) is

$$(2.9) \qquad \phi(x) = ax - \frac{1}{2} bx^2,$$

which has all the properties required by (1.26) as long $x < a/b$. Furthermore, (2.9) implies that $\phi(0) = 0$, which is always possible to have by a suitable construction of the functions in (1.19).

When $\phi(x)$ is given by (2.9), we see that (2.5) and (2.6) give us

$$(2.10) \qquad \hat{x}_1 = \frac{ra + \pi(a-c) + (1-\pi)bS}{(2+r-\pi)b}.$$

We shall consider a numerical example to see how sensitive $\hat{x}_1$ is with respect to the probability of the backstop technology becoming feasible. We shall choose the unit of measurement of the aggregate good so that $\phi'(S) = 1$, i.e. we choose price units so that $p = 1$ gives a demand equal to S.

Furthermore, we assume that the price making demand equal to S/10 is p = 8, i.e. $\phi'(S/10) = 8$. The unit cost of substitute production is assumed to be $c = 1.75$, i.e. almost twice as high as the price making demand equal to S. Finally, we measure the resource by units making $S = 100$. To summarize, we have made the following two assumptions and two choices of measuring units:

$$(2.11) \quad \begin{cases} \left.\begin{array}{l} \phi'(\frac{S}{10}) = 8 \cdot \phi'(S), \\ c = 1,75 \cdot \phi'(S), \end{array}\right\} \text{assumptions} \\ \left.\begin{array}{l} \phi'(S) = 1, \\ S = 100. \end{array}\right\} \text{choice of units} \end{cases}$$

It is easy to see that when $\phi'(x)$ is given by (2.9), (2.11) implies that

$$(2.12) \qquad a = 8 + \frac{7}{9} \quad , \quad b = \frac{7}{90}.$$

With these values of a, b, and c, all our simplifying assumptions in section 1.4 are satisfyed.

To see what $\hat{x}_1$ is for various values of π, we must first choose a value for our discount factor. Usually, the yearly rate of capital return is assumed to lie somewhere between 5% and 10%. In our two-period analysis, it seems reasonable to let each period be longer than one year, the discount factor r must therefore also be larger than what is reasonable for a yearly rate of return. We shall therefore choose $r = 0,5$, which for instance will be the appropriate discount factor if the yearly return on capital is 6% and the average distance between our two periods is 7 years, i.e. the total planning period is 14 years. To get some idea of the importance of what value r has, we shall also consider the limiting case where $r = 0$.

Using the values for a, b and c mentioned above, we find the following values for $\hat{x}_1$ for some values of π:

Optimal resource extraction ($\hat{x}_1$) when c = 1,75
(linear demand function given by (2.7) and (2.12)).

π \ r	0.5	0
0	62.6	50.0
0.25	68.5	55.8
0.5	75.8	63.5
0.75	85.3	74.2
1	97.9	90.4

Table 2.1

We see that in this example there is a considerable increase in $\hat{x}_1$ as π increases. We also see that $\hat{x}_1$ is slightly more affected by π for r=0 than for r=0.5. For any given π, $\hat{x}_1$ is of course lowest for the lowest value of r.

In our numerical example above, the unit cost of substitute production was chosen quite arbitrarily. To see how the value of c affects our results, we have also calculated the optimal resource extraction for c = 0,1, i.e. much lower than the value given by (2.11). The results for c = 0,1 are given in table 2.2.

Optimal resource extraction ($\hat{x}_1$) when c = 0,1
(linear demand function given by (2.7) and (2.12)).

π \ r	0.5	0
0	62.5	50.0
0.25	70.8	58.8
0.5	81.1	70.5
0.75	94.4	86.9
1	100.0	100.0

Table 2.2

Comparing table 2.2 with table 2.1, we see that the optimal resource extraction is more affected by π for the lowest value of c. This is of course what one would expect: In the extreme case with c so high that the backstop technology would not be used even if it was technically feasible, the optimal extraction will be independent of π (cf. also the footnote on page 20). We also see that for c = 0,1, the corner solution $\hat{x}_1 = S$ occurs for π sufficiently high.

2.4. *Log-linear demand function.*

We now assume that

$$(2.13) \qquad \text{Ln } p = \alpha - \beta \text{ Ln } x,$$

where β is positive, i.e.

$$(2.14) \qquad p = \phi'(x) = Ax^{-\beta}$$

where

$$A = e^{\alpha} > 0.$$

The function $\phi(x)$ giving (2.14) is

$$(2.15) \qquad \phi(x) = \frac{A}{1-\beta} x^{1-\beta}$$

which satisfies the properties given by (1.26) as long as $\beta \in (0.1)$, which we shall assume.

When $\phi'(x)$ is given by (2.14), we see that (2.5) and (2.6) gives us the following equation determining $\hat{x}_1$:

$$(2.16) \qquad (1+r)\hat{x}_1^{-\beta} = \pi \frac{c}{A} + (1-\pi)(S-\hat{x}_1)^{-\beta} .$$

It is clear that for $\pi < 1$ a value of $\hat{x}_1 \geqq S$ cannot be a solution to (2.16). The only possibility for the corner solution $\hat{x}_1 = S$ to occur is therefore when $\pi = 1$.

Let us consider the numerical example given by (2.11). Together with (2.14), (2.11) implies that

$$(2.17) \qquad A = 64, \quad \beta = \frac{\text{Ln}8}{\text{Ln}10} .$$

The values for $\hat{x}_1$ following from (2.16) when c = 1,75 are given in table 2.3:

Optimal resource extraction ($\hat{x}_1$) when c = 1,75
(log-linear demand function given by (2.14) and (2.17)).

π \ r	0,5	0
0	61,0	50,0
0,25	63,0	50,5
0,5	65,7	51,2
0,75	70,3	52,2
1	84,3	53,8

Table 2.3

Comparing table 2.3 with table 2.1, we see that in the present case the optimal resource extraction is less affected by the value of π than in the case with the linear demand function. This is particularly true when the discount factor is zero.

When c = 0,1 instead of c = 1,75, the optimal resource extraction is given by table 2.4:

Optimal resource extraction ($\hat{x}_1$) when c = 0,1
(log-linear demand function given by (2.14) and (2.17)).

π \ r	0,5	0
0	61,0	50,0
0,25	68,0	57,5
0,5	76,6	67,4
0,75	87,4	81,3
1	100,0	100,0

Table 2.4

Like in the linear case, we see that the optimal resource extraction is more affected by the value of π for c = 0,1 than for c = 1,75.

2.5. *Summary of chapter 2.*

The optimal resource extraction in the first period is larger the larger is the initial resource stock, the discount factor and the probability of a backstop technology becoming feasible in the second period, and the lower is the cost of producing a substitute, if feasible. The numerical importance of some of these conclusions depends significantly on the values of r and c as well as on the specification of the demand function.

CHAPTER 3.

PERFECT COMPETITION WITH AN UNCERTAIN BACKSTOP TECHNOLOGY.

3.1. General considerations.

In this and the next two chapters we shall consider decision-makers whose objective function is their discounted profits, which we shall denote by V. In the monopoly cases treated in the next chapters there is only one decision-maker, while there of course are several decision-makers in the competitive case. However, to simplify our analysis, we shall assume that all resource extractors in the competitive case are identical in all respects. When this is the case, we can treat all decision-makers together as one decision-maker.

In the beginning of period 1 the decision-maker must choose x_1. Whatever choise of x_1 is made, however, the discounted profits V may take two values: $V^I(x_1)$ if the backstop technology becomes feasible, and $V^{II}(x_1)$ if such a technology does not become feasible. To choose x_1, the decision-maker therefore maximizes EU(V), i.e. the expected value of some concave function of V (cf. section 1.3, pp. 16 - 17). From the definition of $V^I(x_1)$ and $V^{II}(x_2)$ we have

$$(3.1) \qquad EU(V) = \pi U(V^I(x_1)) + (1-\pi)U(V^{II}(x_1)),$$

and

$$(3.2) \qquad \frac{dEU(V)}{dx_1} = \pi U'(V^I(x_1)) \cdot \frac{dV^I(x_1)}{dx_1} + (1-\pi)U'(V^{II}(x_1))\frac{dV^{II}(x_1)}{dx_1}.$$

The function EU(V) will always be concave due to our assumptions (1.25) and (1.26). The following conditions are therefore necessary and sufficient for $\hat{x}_1$ to maximize EU(V):

$$(3.3)\quad \begin{cases} \pi U'(V^{I}(\hat{x}_1))\,\dfrac{dV^{I}(\hat{x}_1)}{dx_1} + (1-\pi)\,U'(V^{II}(\hat{x}_1))\cdot\dfrac{dV^{II}(\hat{x}_1)}{dx_1} = 0 \\ \text{or } \hat{x}_1 = 0 \text{ and } \pi U'(V^{I}(0))\,\dfrac{dV^{I}(0)}{dx_1} + (1-\pi)U'(V^{II}(0))\,\dfrac{dV^{II}(0)}{dx_1} \leqq 0 \\ \text{or } \hat{x}_1 = S \text{ and } \pi U'(V^{I}(S))\,\dfrac{dV^{I}(S)}{dx_1} + (1-\pi)U'(V^{II}(S))\,\dfrac{dV^{II}(S)}{dx_1} \geqq 0 \end{cases}$$

Let us now define a function $\pi^*(x_1)$, where $\pi^*\in[0,1]$ whatever value x_1 has, by the following equation:

$$(3.4)\qquad \frac{\pi^*(x_1)}{1-\pi^*(x_1)} = \frac{\pi U'(V^{I}(x_1))}{(1-\pi)U'(V^{II}(x_1))}\,.$$

If we know the value of $\pi^*(\hat{x}_1)$, it is clear that $\hat{x}_1$ could be found simply by maximizing EV with π substituted by $\pi^*(\hat{x}_1)$, i.e. by maximizing

$$(3.5)\qquad EV^* = \pi^*(\hat{x}_1)V^{I}(x_1) + (1-\pi^*(\hat{x}_1))V^{II}(x_1).$$

It is easy to see, using (3.4), that the value of x_1 which maximizes (3.5) is identical to $\hat{x}_1$ from (3.3).

The importance of the procedure above is the following: Assume that the sign of $U'(V^{I}(\hat{x}_1)) - U'(V^{II}(\hat{x}_1))$ is known, for instance positive. Then we know from (3.4) that $\pi < \pi^*(\hat{x}_1) < 1$. If we want to compare $\hat{x}_1$ when we have risk aversion ,and know that $U'(V^{I}(\hat{x}_1)) > U'(V^{II}(\hat{x}_1))$ in this case, with $\hat{x}_1$ when the decision-maker is risk neutral, we can simply compare solutions to the problem of maximizing EV* for different values of π^*. In the case with risk neutrality we must have $\pi^* = \pi$, while $\pi^* > \pi$ if $U''(V) < 0$.

Alternatively stated, we can say that introducing risk aversion instead of risk neutrality has the same affect on $\hat{x}_1$ as an increase of the probability of the state of the world which the decision-maker regards as least desirable. In the example above this state of the world is the state where a backstop technology has become feasible.

In the proceeding sections we shall use this result to show in which case ($U''(V) = 0$ or $U''(V) < 0$) the resource extraction in period 1 is largest.

3.2 The general case.

As we mentioned in the preceding section, we shall reason as if we only have one decision-maker. The discounted profit of this resource extracting firm is given by

$$(3.6) \qquad V = p(1)x_1 + (1+r)^{-1}\, p(2)(S-x_1),$$

where the decision-maker considers the price in period 1 and 2, p(1) and p(2), to be unaffected by his own actions. The uncertainty concerning the feasibility of a backstop technology will make the competitive firm uncertain about the price in period 2. If a backstop technology becomes feasible, the price is expected to be $p^{I}(2)$, otherwise it is expected to be $p^{II}(2)$, This means that even for a given x_1, V will not be known with certainty.

The functions $V^{I}(x_1)$ and $V^{II}(x_2)$ introdused in the preceding section are now given by

$$V^{I}(x_1) = p(1)x_1 + (1+r)^{-1}p^{I}(2)(S-x_1),$$

(3.7)

$$V^{II}(x_1) = p(1)x_1 + (1+r)^{-1}p^{II}(2)(S-x_1).$$

From our reasoning in section 3.1 it is clear that maximization of EU(V), where U is some concave function, is the same as maximizing

$$EV^* = p(1)x_1 + (1+r)^{-1}(S - x_1)(\pi^* p^{I}(2) + (1-\pi^*)p^{II}(2)), \tag{3.8}$$

for some value of π^*, where we have used (3.5) and (3.7). It is clear that a value of $x_1 \in (0,S)$ will maximize (3.8) if and only if

$$\pi^* p^{I}(2) + (1-\pi^*)p^{II}(2) = (1+r)p(1). \tag{3.9}$$

If $\pi^* = \pi$, which will be the case if the competitive firm is risk neutral, (3.9) states that the expected value of p(2) is equal to (1+r)p(1). A similar result has been derived in problems with other types of uncertainty, see for instance Heal (1975, pp. 125-130), Hoel (1978c, pp. 640-1), and Weinstein and Zeckhauser (1975, pp. 381-386). When $\pi = \pi^*$ it is also easy to see that (3.9) is a special case of an equation used by Dasgupta and Stiglitz (1976, equation (1.1)). We shall return to the case where $\pi^* \neq \pi$ shortly, but first show what the equilibrium prices will be.

The equilibrium price in period 1 is determined by

$$p(1) = \phi'(x_1). \tag{3.10}$$

The equilibrium price in period 2 depends on whether or not substitute production becomes possible. If such production does *not* become possible, we must have

$$p^{II}(2) = \phi'(S-x_1). \tag{3.11}$$

If the backstop technology becomes possible, $p(2)$ cannot exceed c. Furthermore, $p(2) < c$ is not a possible equilibrium price, because in this case we would have $x_2 = 0$, so that $p(t)$ would be determined by (3.11) even if substitute production was technically feasible. But if $p(2)$ is determined by (3.11) whether or not a backstop technology becomes feasible, it is easy to see that $x_1 \geqq S/2$ in equilibrium. But this means that $p(2) = \phi'(S-x_1) \geqq \phi'(S/2) > c$ (cf. (1.28)) in equilibrium. This contradiction proves that $p(2) < c$ is not possible. We therefore must have

$$(3.12) \qquad p^I(2) = c \ .$$

Inserting (3.10) - (3.12) into (3.9) gives us

$$(3.13) \qquad \pi^*c + (1-\pi^*)\phi'(S - x_1) = (1+r)\phi'(x_1).$$

If $\pi^* = \pi$ we see that the equilibrium value of x_1 obtained by (3.13) is identical to the social optimum $\hat{x}_1$ from (2.5) when $\partial EZ/\partial x_1 = 0$.

Let us now assume that our competitive firm has risk avertion, i.e. that $U(V)$ is strictly concave. We argued above that $p^I(2) < p^{II}(2)$, so that (3.7) gives us $V^I(x_1) < V^{II}(x_1)$ for the relevant values of x_1. Because $U''(V) < 0$, we therefore must have $U'(V^I(x_1)) > U'(V^{II}(x_1))$. From (3.4) and our reasoning in the end of section 3.1 it is therefore clear that the appropriate π^* in our present case is larger than π. Now (3.13) is identical to (2.5) except that π is substituted by π^*, and our reasoning in connection with (2.5) and figure 2.1 demonstrated that $\hat{x}_1$ was higher the higher was π. This means that the competitive solution has a higher resource extraction in period 1 than what is socially optimal when the resource extractors have risk aversion.

Se far we have disregard the possibility of corner solutions. However, from our reasoning above it is clear that the competitive solution may give $\hat{x}_1 = S$ even when this resource extraction is higher than what is socially optimal. The opposite can, however, not occur: If $\hat{x}_1 = S$ is socially optimal, the competitive solution will give us this solution for any concave function $U(V)$.

We mentioned above that for $\pi^* = \pi$ we got $E[p(2)/p(1)] = 1+r$. The general formula for $E[p(2)/p(1)]$ is given by

$$(3.14) \qquad E[p(2)/p(1)] = \frac{\pi p^{I}(2) + (1-\pi)p^{II}(2)}{p(1)} \quad .$$

When the competitive firm has risk aversion, we saw that this implies $\pi^* > \pi$. Furthermore, we have shown that $p^{I}(2) < p^{II}(2)$, so that (3.14) implies that

$$(3.15) \qquad E[p(2)/p(1)] > \frac{\pi^* p^{I}(2) + (1-\pi^*)p^{II}(2)}{p(1)} \quad .$$

Disregarding corner solutions, (3.13) and (3.15) therefore imply that

$$(3.16) \qquad E[p(2)/p(1)] > 1+r \ ,$$

i.e. that the expected rate of price increase exceeds the discount factor. Again, this is in accordance with the results referred to after equation (3.9).

We have shown that the *expected* rate of price increase will always be at least as large as the discount factor. The *actual* rate of price change will of course depend on which state of the world one gets in the second period. If the backstop technology does *not* become feasible, it follows from our result above as well as the fact that $p^{II}(2) > p^{I}(2)$ that the price increase in this case always must exceed the discount factor. On the other hand, if the backstop technology *does* become feasible, the rate of price change will always be less than the discount factor. This follows from figure 2.1, which always has $(1+r)\phi'(\hat{x}_1) > c$, which together with (3.10) and (3.12) gives us $p^{I}(2) < (1+r)p(1)$. Actually, we may even find that $p^{I}(2) < p(1)$, i.e. that the price becomes lower in period 2 than it was in period 1.

Dasgupta and Stiglitz (1976, pp. 20-24) have showed how the resource price develops in the continuous time case when the firms are risk neutral. In this case p(t) rises with the rate r till the date when the backstop technology becomes feasible. At this date the price drops to some value lower than c, and then continues to grow with the rate r until p(t) reaches c, which occurs exactly when the resource is totally depleted. In the period before the backstop technology becomes available, the price, which is rising with the rate r, may be below c all the time, may start below c and reach a value higher than c, or may be higher than c all the time. In our case, the possibility of $p(1) > c$ corresponds to some kind of average value of p(t) in the period before the backstop technology becomes available being higher than c.

3.3. Linear and log-linear demand functions.

We have seen that for any given π the competitive solution coincides with the solution which would be socially optimal if the probability of a backstop technology becoming available was π^*, where $\pi^* \geqq \pi$ and equality holds if and only if the competitive firms are risk neutral. The competitive solution when the demand function is linear or log-linear therefore follows directly from sections 2.3 and 2.4. For instance, assume that the demand function is linear with coefficients given by (2.12), and that $\pi = 0.25$. For $r = 0.5$ the optimal solution given by table 2.1 is $\hat{x}_1 = 68.5$. Let us assume that the function $U(V)$ of the competitive firm implies that $\pi^* = 0.75$. From table 2.1 we see that the resource extraction in the competitive solution is $\hat{x}_1 = 85.3$, i.e. considerably higher than what is socially optimal.

The welfare loss of the competitive solution with risk aversion can be measured by comparing Z given by (2.1) for $x_1 = 68.5$ and $x_1 = 85.3$. Now Z depends of course not only on x_1, but also on whether or not a backstop technology becomes feasible in period 2. Actually, it is easy to see that *if* such a technology becomes available, the competitive solution for $\hat{x}_1$ will give a higher value of Z than the optimal solution for x_1 would give. But at the time x_1 must be chosen, one does not know whether or not substitute production will be possible. The only meaningful comparison between the two cases is therefore between the expected values of Z.

The expression for EZ follows from (2.4). The function $\hat{x}_2(x_1)$ enters this expression, and from (2.3) and (2.8) we see that

$$(3.17) \quad \hat{x}_2(x_1) = \frac{a-c}{b} - S + x_1.$$

Inserting (3.17) and (2.9) into (2.4) gives us

$$(3.18) \qquad EZ = ax_1 - \frac{1}{2}bx_1^2$$

$$+ (1+r)^{-1}\pi[a\frac{a-c}{b} - \frac{b}{2}(\frac{a-c}{b})^2$$

$$- c\,(\frac{a-c}{b} - S + x_1)]$$

$$+ (1+r)^{-1}(1-\pi)[a(S-x_1) - \frac{b}{2}(S-x_1)^2].$$

Denoting the optimal value of EZ, i.e. when $x_1 = 68.5$, by EZ^o, and the value of EZ in the competitive case, i.e. when $x_1 = 85.3$, by EZ^c, we obtain, by inserting $r = 0.5$, $c = 1.75$ and (2.12) into (3.18):

$$(3.19) \qquad \begin{cases} EZ^o = 634.2. \\ EZ^c = 583.3. \end{cases}$$

This means that the welfare loss is 8% of the optimal expected value of Z, i.e. quite a significant loss in this example.

To see how realistic this example is, let us check how strong a degree of risk aversion the example assumes. A measure of relative risk aversion is (cf. Arrow (1965) and Pratt (1964)).

$$(3.20) \qquad R_R(V) = \frac{-VU''(V)}{U'(V)}.$$

Let us as a simplification assume that $R_R(V)$ is constant over the relevant area of V. In this case the function U(V) may be written

(3.21) $$U(V) = \frac{B}{1-\rho} V^{1-\rho}$$

over the relevant area of V, where $\rho \neq 1$ and ρ and B are positive constants. We see that (3.20) and (3.21) give us $R_R(V) = \rho$. To find the implised value of ρ, we can use (3.4), which together with (3.21) gives us

(3.22) $$\left[\frac{V^{I}(\hat{x}_1)}{V^{II}(\hat{x}_1)}\right]^{-\rho} = \frac{\pi^*}{1-\pi^*}\,\frac{1-\pi}{\pi} = \frac{0{,}75}{0{,}25}\cdot\frac{0{,}75}{0{,}25} = 9.$$

For $\hat{x}_1 = 85{,}3$, we see from (3.7), (3.10) and (3.11) that we in our present case have

$$V^{I}(\hat{x}_1) = (a-b\hat{x}_1)\hat{x}_1 + (1+r)^{-1}c(S-\hat{x}_1) = 199{,}98$$

and

$$V^{II}(\hat{x}_1) = (a-b\hat{x}_1)\hat{x}_1 + (1+r)^{-1}(a-bS+b\hat{x}_1)(S-\hat{x}_1) = 257{,}64$$

which gives us

$$\rho = -\frac{\text{Ln } 9}{\text{Ln}\left[\frac{199{,}98}{257{,}64}\right]} = 8{,}67.$$

In other words, our example is based on a quite high degree of risk aversion. If the relative risk aversion is closer to one, the welfare loss of the competitive case will not be as large as we indicated above.

To see the importance of the demand function, we could calculate EZ^o and EZ^c in a similar way as we did in (3.16) when the demand function is log-linear. We shall not go through this in detail, but it is easy to see that the welfare loss must be much smaller in this case than when the demand function is linear: The welfare loss of the competitive solution can obviously not exceed the loss which would occur in the limiting extreme situation where $\pi = 0$, but where the competitive firms maximize EV* using $\pi^* = 1$. The loss in this situation is easily calculated by inserting $x_1 = 61.0$ and $x_1 = 84.3$ (for r=0.5, cf. table 2.3) into (2.1) when $x_2 = 0$ and $\phi(x)$ is given by (2.15), with A=64 and β=Ln8/Ln10. This loss, in per cent of Z when $x_1 = 61.0$, is 1.37%, i.e. much lower than the welfare loss we found when the demand function was linear. With r=0 we would find that even if $\pi = 0$ and the competitive forms used $\pi^* = 1$ the welfare loss would be practically zero in the case with a log-linear demand function.

3.4. Summary of chapter 3.

We have shown that if it is socially optimal not to extract all of the resource in the first period, the resource extraction under perfect competition will be socially optimal if the firms are risk neutral. If the firms have risk aversion, there will be too much resource extraction in the first period under perfect competition. If it is socially optimal to extract all of the resource in the first period, perfect competition will always give this result under the assumptions we have made.

The numerical importance of the result mentioned above depends on the form of the demand function. We saw that the welfare loss would be extremely small when the demand function was log-linear, while it could be more significant when the demand function was linear.

For reasons mentioned in section 1.3, we have defined the socially optimal value of x_1 as the value maximizing EZ. If we instead maximized EU(Z) where U was some strictly concave function of Z, we would generally get a different social optimum. Using the same reasoning as we did in section 3.1, it is clear that the optimal value of x_1 in this case can be found by maximizing

$$EZ^* = \phi(x_1)+(1+r)^{-1}\pi^*(\phi(S-x_1+\hat{x}_2(x_1))-c\hat{x}_2(x_1))+(1+r)^{-1}(1-\pi^*)\phi(S-x_1), \qquad (3.23)$$

where $\hat{x}_2(x_1)$ like before is given by (2.3), for some π^*. Now it is clear from section (2.2) that the most desirable state of the world, from society's point of view, is that a backstop technology *does* become feasible. Risk aversion for the society therefore means that π^* in (3.22) is smaller than the true probability π. The consequence of this is that compared with the optimal solution with risk neutrality, we now get a lower resource extraction in the first period. In other words, our conclusion about too much resource extraction under competitive conditions is strengthened if the society has risk aversion. A similar argument is given by Hoel (1978c) for the case where it is the cost of producing the substitute that is uncertain.

CHAPTER 4.

FULL MONOPOLY WITH AN UNCERTAIN BACKSTOP TECHNOLOGY.

4.1. The general case.

In our general discussion in section 3.1 we found that any profit maximizing firm would maximize

$$EV^* = \pi^* V^I(x_1) + (1 - \pi^*) V^{II}(x_1),$$

where π^* is given by (3.4) for $x_1 = \hat{x}_1$.[1)]

When a single monopolist controls all resource extraction as well as substitute production, if feasible, $V^I(x_1)$ and $V^{II}(x_1)$ are given by the following formulas (using 1.20)):

$$(4.1) \qquad V^I(x_1) = x_1\phi'(x_1) + (1 + r)^{-1} m(x_1)$$

where

$$(4.2) \qquad m(x_1) = \underset{x_2 \geq 0}{\text{Max}}[(S - x_1 + x_2)\phi'(S - x_1 + x_2) - c\, x_2],$$

and

$$(4.3) \qquad V^{II}(x_1) = x_1\phi'(x_1) + (1 + r)^{-1}\phi'(S - x_1).$$

1) For notational convenience, we shall use π^* instead of $\pi^*(\hat{x}_1)$.

We obviously must have $m(x_1) \geqq \phi'(S - x_1)$, as the monopolist always has the option of choosing $x_2 = 0$. We would get $m(x_1) = \phi'(S - x_1)$ if and only if the marginal revenue of increasing x_2 from zero does not exceed c, i.e.[1)]

$$(4.4) \qquad m(x_1) = \phi'(S - x_1) \Leftrightarrow \phi'(S - x_1) + (S - x_1)\phi''(S - x_1) \leqq c.$$

Let us first treat the case where it turns out that when x_1 is chosen optimally, we get $m(x_1) = \phi'(S - x_1)$. In this case the monopolist is indifferent as to whether the backstop technology becomes feasible or not, and the value of x_1 which maximizes EV* will therefore be independent of π^*. It is easy to derive that the optimal value of x_1 in this case is given by

$$(4.5) \qquad (1+r)[\phi'(\hat{x}_1)+\hat{x}_1\phi''(\hat{x}_1)] = \phi'(S-\hat{x}_1) + (S-\hat{x}_1)\phi''(S-\hat{x}_1).$$

Because $r \geqq 0$ and $x\phi'(x)$ is strictly concave in x, the solution following from (4.5) must satisfy $\hat{x}_1 \geqq S/2$, where the equality sign holds if and only if $r = 0$.

Let us now turn to the more interesting case where $m(x_1) > \phi'(S-x_1)$ when x_1 is chosen optimally, i.e. where the monopolist has advantage of the backstop technology becoming feasible. From (4.2) it is easy to see that when $m(x_1) > \phi'(S-x_1)$, which implies $x_2 > 0$, we obtain $m'(x_1) = -c$. Using this we find that the optimal solution in this case must be given by

$$(4.6) \qquad (1+r)[\phi'(\hat{x}_1) + \hat{x}_1\phi''(\hat{x}_1)] = f(x_1,\pi^*)$$

where

1)The "if" part of this statement, i.e. the implication "$\Leftarrow$" in (4.4), follows from our assumption that $x\phi'(x)$ is concave in x (cf. (1.26)).

(4.7) $$\tilde{f}(x_1,\pi) = \pi^*c+(1-\pi^*)[\phi'(S-\hat{x}_1)+(S-\hat{x}_1)\phi''(S-\hat{x}_1)].$$

This solution may be illustrated by a similar figure as we used when analyzing the social optimum (cf. figure 2.1). In fact, figure 4.1 is identical to figure 2.1 except that $\phi'(x)$ has been substituted by $\phi'(x)+x\phi''(x)$ and that $f(x_1,\pi)$ has been substituted by $\tilde{f}(x_1,\pi)$. Like in the competitive case, the decreasing fully drawn curve and the in-

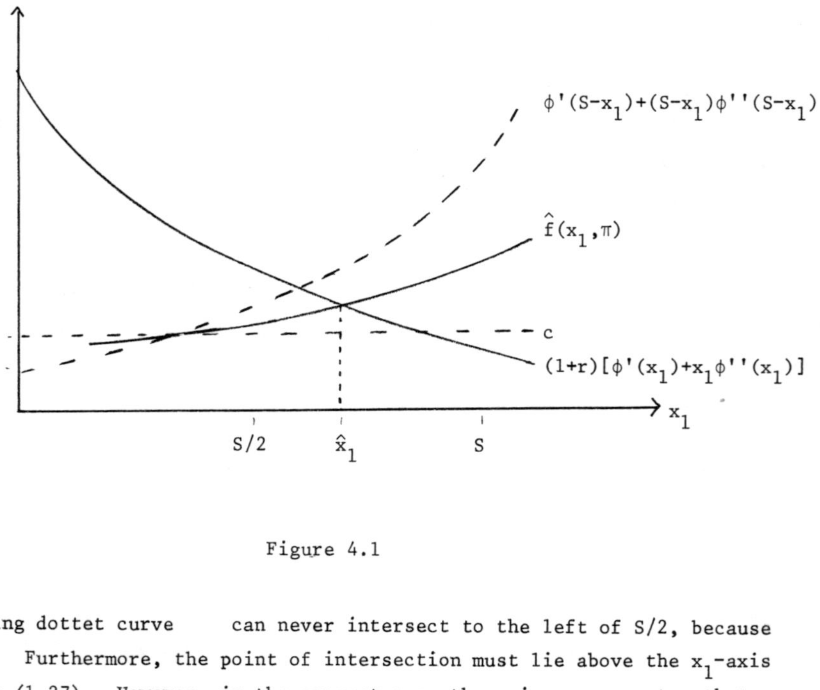

Figure 4.1

creasing dottet curve can never intersect to the left of S/2, because $r \geq 0$. Furthermore, the point of intersection must lie above the x_1-axis due to (1.27). However, in the present case there is no guarantee that this intersection point will be above the c-line. If the intersection point is below the c-line, the solution given by (4.6) would imply that the intersection between the two fully drawn curves was to the left of the intersection point first mentioned. But in this case we would get $\phi'(S-\hat{x}_1)+(S-\hat{x}_1)\phi''(S-\hat{x}_1) < c$, so that it would *not* be the solution given by (4.6) that was valid in this case. The solution given by (4.5) would be the correct solution in this case, as this solution is given by the intersection between the fully drawn decreasing curve and the dotted increasing curve, and is valid when this intersection point lies below the c-line (cf. (4.4)). In figure 4.2 we have drawn an example of the case where the intersection of the two curves lies below the c-line, and the solution given by (4.5) therefore is valid.

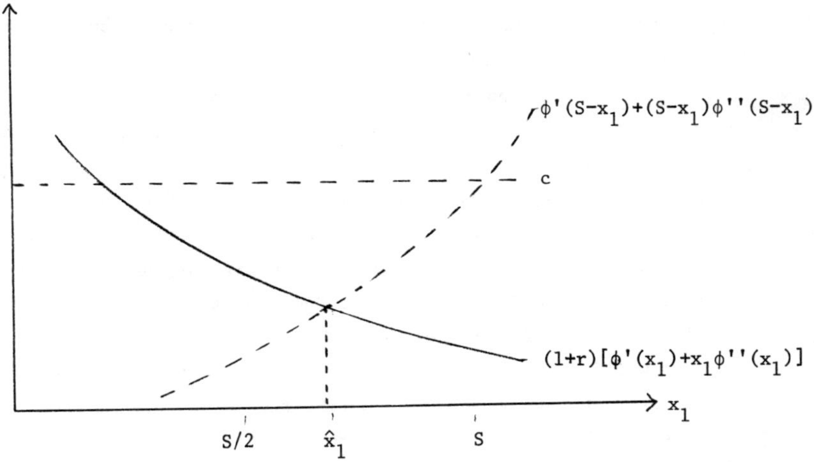

Figure 4.2

Like before, we of course find that $\hat{x}_1$ is larger the larger is S and the larger is r, as long as we do not have a corner solution. However, in the case of social optimun and perfect competition we found that $\hat{x}_1$ always increased with π^* (or π in the case of social optimum) as long as $\hat{x}_1 < S$. In the present case this is not necessarily so. If c is so high that the solution is given by (4.5), $\hat{x}_1$ will be unaffected by π^*. But *if* $\hat{x}_1$ is affected, we see that $\hat{x}_1$ must increase with π^* also in the present case.

From our reasoning after (4.3), we know that unless the monopolist regards both the two states of the world as equally desirable, he regards the situation where the backstop technology *does* become feasible as the most desirable alternative. From our discussion in section 3.1, this means that risk aversion will imply that $\pi^* < \pi$ if our soultion is given by (4.6), and therefore affected by π^*. In other words, if the monopolist's optimal extraction depends on the probability of the backstop technology becoming feasible, the monopolist will extract less in period 1 if he has risk aversion than he would if he was risk neutral. This result is the opposite of what we found in the competitive case. The reason for this difference is that while the competitive firms regarded substitute production as a source of increased supply depressing the resource price, the monopolist regards the feasibility of substitute production as an opportunity which he may or may not utilize, depending on what is most profitable. In other words, it is the fact that the monopolist is assumed to control the backstop technology which makes the situation different from the competitive case. It follows from this that one would expect a resource monopoly *not* controlling the backstop technology to behave in a way more like the competitive market. We shall see in the next chapter that this in fact is the case.

So far we have not compared the resource extraction in the case of monopoly with the resource extraction in the competitive case, using the same value of π^* in both cases. Intuitively, one would probably expect the monopolist to extract less in the first period than the competitive firms. However, this is not necessarily the case. Comparisons between the monopolistic and the competitive case when there is no backstop technology (i.e. $\pi^*=0$) have been given by Kay and Mirrlees (1975), Lewis (1977), Stiglitz (1976), Sweeney (1977) and Weinsten and Zeckhauser (1975).

Obviously, both the competitive and the monopolistic resource extraction in period 1 will be S/2 if $r=\pi=0$. Let us therefore turn to the case where $r \geqq 0$ and $\pi^* \geqq 0$, with one strict inequality holding, and compare the monopolistic and competitive case when π^* is the same in both cases. Define the demand elasticity (measured positively) as

$$(4.8) \qquad \eta(x) = \left[\frac{-\phi''(x)x}{\phi'(x)}\right]^{-1}.$$

Notice that $\eta(x) > 0$ because $\phi''(x) < 0$ and that $\eta(x) > 1$ for $x \leqq S/2$ because of (1.27). The monopolistic solution is given either by (4.5) or (4.6). These equations may be rewritten by using (4.8), giving

$$(4.9) \qquad \left[1-\frac{1}{\eta(\hat{x}_1)}\right](1+r)\phi'(\hat{x}_1) = \left[1-\frac{1}{\eta(S-\hat{x}_1)}\right]\phi'(S-\hat{x}_1)$$

and

$$(4.10) \qquad \left[1-\frac{1}{\eta(\hat{x}_1)}\right](1+r)\phi'(\hat{x}_1) = \pi^*c + (1-\pi^*)\left[1-\frac{1}{\eta(S-\hat{x}_1)}\right]\phi'(S-\hat{x}_1),$$

respectively. From (4.9) and (4.10) it is clear that unless $r=0$, which may give $\hat{x}_1 = S/2$, i.e. less extraction than the competitive solution, we find $\hat{x}_1 > S/2$. Let us now assume that the demand function has a price elasticity which is higher the higher the price is, i.e. $\eta'(x_1) < 0$. Then $\hat{x}_1 > S/2$ implies $\eta(\hat{x}_1) < \eta(S-\hat{x}_1)$. If the monopoly solution is given by (4.9), this gives us

$$(4.11) \qquad (1+r)\phi'(\hat{x}_1) > \phi'(S-\hat{x}_1).$$

But comparing this inequality with figure 2.1, which gave us the optimal and competitive solution, it is clear that the initial resource extraction in the monopolistic case must be lower than in the competitive case. Similarly, if the monopolistic solution is given by (4.10), $\hat{x}_1 > S/2$ and $\eta'(x_1) < 0$ imply

$$(4.12) \qquad (1+r)\phi'(\hat{x}_1) > \pi^*c+(1-\pi^*)\phi'(S-\hat{x}_1) = f(\hat{x}_1,\pi^*).$$

Together with figure 2.1 it is clear that this inequality implies that the initial resource extraction under monopoly must be lower than the compatitive extraction.

We have seen that when π^* is the same in both cases, a *sufficient* condition for the monopoly case to have a lower extraction than the competitive case is that the demand elasticity is higher the higher the price is.[1] Whatever the relationship between these two market structures are with the same π^*, it is probably more interesting to compare the two cases for the some π, which only implies the same π^* if there is risk neutrality in both cases. If we assume that there is risk aversion both in the competitive and the monopolistic case, we have seen that this tends to make the resource extraction in the first period lower in the monopolistic case than in the competitive case.

This effect may well be stronger than the possible effect of the resource extraction being highest in the monopolistic case for the some π^*.

We shall not use more space on possible relationships between these two market structures as well as the socially optimal extraction in the general case, but rather turn to our two examples of demand functions.

---

1) It is straightforward to show that we can substitute the requirement $\eta'(x) < 0$ by $\eta'(x) \leqq 0$ if $\pi^* > 0$.

4.2. Linear demand function.

Assume now that the demand function is given by (2.8). In this case the solution (4.5) gives us

$$(1+r)(a-2b\hat{x}_1) = a-2b(S-\hat{x}_1).$$

Alternatively written, we have

$$(4.13) \qquad \hat{x}_1 = \frac{ra+2bS}{(2+r)2b},$$

unless this gives a value exceeding S. From (4.4) it is clear that this solution, which is independent of π^*, is valid if and only if

$$(4.14) \qquad a-2b(S-\hat{x}_1) \leqq c$$

with (4.13) inserted. From our assumption that $c < a$ we can therefore disregard $\hat{x}_1 = S$. Inserting (4.13) into (4.14) therefore gives us, after some manipulation, the following inequality:

$$(4.15) \qquad a - \frac{2+r}{2+2r}c \leqq bS.$$

If and only if (4.15) holds the optimal resource extraction is given by (4.13).

When (4.15) does *not* hold, our solution is given by (4.6), which in the case of our linear demand function may be written

$$(1+r)(a-2b\hat{x}_1) = \pi^*c+(1-\pi^*)[a-2b(S-\hat{x}_1)]$$

as long as the value of $\hat{x}_1$ following from this equation does not exceed S. When (4.15) does not hold and $\hat{x}_1 = S$ is disregarded the optimal solution is therefore given by

$$(4.16) \qquad \hat{x}_1 = \frac{ra+\pi^*(a-c)+(1-\pi^*)2bS}{(2+r-\pi^*)2b} .$$

When the demand function is given by (2.5), the elasticity $\eta(x)$ defined by (4.8) becomes

$$\eta(x) = \frac{a}{bx} - 1,$$

i.e. $\eta'(x) < 0$. From our general discussion in section 4.1 (pp. 184-6) we therefore can conclude that the resource extraction in the first period under full monopoly is always less than what it is both in the competitive solution and in the social optimum. The only two exceptions are when $r = \pi^* = 0$ and when $\hat{x}_1 = S$ in the monopoly case, in these cases all three solutions will be identical

This conclusion corresponds to what was found in Hoel (1978a, pp. 18-24) in the case where substitute production was technically possible from the initial time point. In this case it was shown that with a linear demand function the initial resource extraction would be lower for a monopolist than it would be under competitive conditions. The present analysis has shown that this conclusion is valid also when the posibility of substitute production is uncertain, at least under the simplifying assumptions we have used.

Let us now turn to our numerical example. When our parameters are given by (2.11) and (2.12), it is easy to verify that (4.15) holds, both for $r = 0,5$ and $r = 0$. The optimal resource extraction is therefore independent of π^*, and from (4.13) we find that $\hat{x}_1 = 51,3$ for $r = 0,5$ and $r = 50,0$ for $r = 0$. Comparing these results with table 2.1, we see that the monopoly results differ quite significantly from what we found for the social optimum and the competitive case. In the latter cases we found that the values of both π (or π^*) and r were important in determining the level of resource extraction. The monopoly solution, on the other hand, is unaffected by π^* and only slightly affected by r. A consequence of this difference is that if the probability of a backstop technology becoming feasible is large, i.e. π close to one, the resource extraction of the monopolist in the first period will be considerably lower than what is socially optimal. For instance, if $r = 0,5$ and $\pi = 0,75$, it will be socially optimal to extract 85,3% of the resource in the first period, while the monopolist will extract only 51,3%. The welfare loss of this can be calculated in the same way as we did in section 3.3. We shall not go through this calculation, but our numerical values from section 3.3 indicate that this welfare loss may be of significant importance.

If we instead of $c = 1,75$ assume that $c = 0,1$, we find that (4.15) is not valid whatever non-negative discount factor we use. The solution is therefore found by using (4.16), and is given in table 4.1.

Resource extraction ($\hat{x}_1$) with full monopoly when $c = 0,1$ (linear demand function given by (2.7) and (2.12).

π^* \ r	0,5	0
0	51,3	50,0
0,25	52,1	50,8
0,5	53,1	51,9
0,75	54,3	53,5
1	56,0	55,8

Table 4.1

From table 4.1 we see the resource extraction by the monopolist is quite insensitive both to the value of π^* and r. Comparing this result with table 2.2, we see that also for c = 0,1 this result is quite different from what we found for the social optimum and the competitive case.

4.3. Log-linear demand function.

When the demand function is given by (2.14), we see that

$$(4.17) \qquad \phi'(x) + x\phi''(x) = (1-\beta)\phi'(x) = (1-\beta)Ax^{-\beta}.$$

Inserting this into (4.5) gives us

$$(4.18) \qquad (1+r)\hat{x}_1^{-\beta} = (S-\hat{x}_1)^{-\beta},$$

which is valid when the inequality in (4.4) holds, i.e. when

$$(4.19) \qquad (1-\beta)A(S-\hat{x}_1)^{-\beta} \leqq c,$$

with $\hat{x}_1$ given by (4.18). For $\hat{x}_1$ sufficiently close to S (4.19) cannot be valid, the solution $\hat{x}_1 = S$ will therefore never follow from (4.18).

When (4.19) is not valid, the solution follows from (4.6), which in the present case can be written

$$(4.20) \qquad (1+r)\hat{x}_1^{-\beta} = \pi^*\frac{c}{(1-\beta)A} + (1-\pi^*)(S-\hat{x}_1)^{-\beta}.$$

From this equation it is clear that $\hat{x}_1 = S$ can only be a solution if $\pi^* = 1$.

Let us first look at the case when there is no chance of a backstop technology becoming feasible, i.e. $\pi=0$. From the definition of π^* (see (3.4)) it follows that $\pi^* = 0$ in this case. Comparing (4.18) and (4.20), we see that these two solutions are identical when $\pi^* = 0$, so that the monopolist's resource extraction is given by (4.18) when $\pi^*=0$. The socially optimal extraction, equal to the extraction under competitive conditions in this case folowws from (2.16) with $\pi=0$. By comparing these two solutions we see that the resource extraction following from full monopoly is identical to the competitive and socially optimal extraction. This consequence following from a log-linear demand function has been mentioned by several economists, see for instance Lewis (1977), Stiglitz (1976), Sweeney (1977) and Weinstein and Zeckhauser (1975).

We now turn to the case where π and π^* are positive. In this case it follows from our general discussion in section 4.1 (pp. 48 - 50) that the resource extraction in the first period under full monopoly is always less than what it is both in the competitive solution and in the social optimum. This conclusion holds both for the case of risk neutrality and for the case of risk aversion. When there is risk neutrality a similar result has been given by Dasgupta & Stiglitz (1976, pp. 30-37): They show that when time is continuous, the initial resource extraction is lower under full monopoly than the socially optimal extraction.

Let us now turn to our numerical example, with parameters given by (2.11) and (2.17). When $r = 0,5$ we find that (4.18) gives us $\hat{x}_1 = 61,0$. Inserted into (4.19), we find that this inequality holds for this value of $\hat{x}_1$. This means that for $r = 0,5$ the solution to the monopolist's optimization problem is independent of π^*, and given by $\hat{x}_1 = 61,0$. It turns out that also when $r = 0$ the correct solution follows from (4.18), giving us $\hat{x}_1 = 50,0$ whatever value π^* has. Comparing these results with table 2.3, we see that when $r = 0$ the difference between the monopoly solution and the social optimum is quite small, whatever value π has. When $r = 0,5$, however, the difference between the two solutions becomes quite significant, just like we found in the case with a linear demand function.

When c = 0,1, we find by using (4.18) that with the value of $\hat{x}_1$ following from this equation both for r = 0,5 and r = 0 the inequality given by (4.19) does not hold. This mean that when c = 0,1 the solution $\hat{x}_1$ follows from (4.20), the solutions for different values of π^* and r are given in table 4.2.

Resource extraction ($\hat{x}_1$) with full monopoly when c = 0,1 (log-linear demand function given by (2.14) and (2.17).

π^* \ r	0,5	0
0	61,0	50,0
0,25	65,2	53,6
0,5	71,0	58,5
0,75	79,9	66,5
1	100,0	96,6

Table 4.2

From this table we see that when c = 0,1, the value of π^* has a significant influence on the determination of the resource extraction. Like in earlier cases, however, this influence is smaller than it is for the socially optimal resource extraction, see table 2.4.

4.4. Summary of chapter 4.

In chapter 3 we saw that the initial resource extraction under competition always would be higher the higher the probability of a backstop technology becoming available was (disregarding corner solutions). In the case of full monopoly, treated in the present chapter, this was not always so. For a sufficiently high cost of producing the substitute the monopolist would not take the backstop technology into use although this would be socially desirable. In this case the monopolist's initial resource extraction was of course independent of the probability of substitute production becoming technically feasible. However, if the cost of producing the substitute is sufficiently low to make it profitable for the monopolist to use the backstop technology, if technically feasible, the monopolist's initial resource extraction will be higher the higher is the probability of the backstop technology becoming available. In other words, in this case we get a result similar to what we found for the social optimum and the competitive solution.

If the monopolist's initial resource extraction depends on the probability of the backstop technology becoming available, risk aversion will imply a lower initial resource extraction than one would get if the monopolist was risk neutral. This conclusion is the opposite of what we found in the competitive case.

One cannot conclude that the present monopolistic case always will have a lower initial resource extraction than the competitive or the socially optimal solution. However, this will be the case for most reasonable specifications of the demand function, especially when the resource extracting monopoly - or resource extracting firms in the case of competition - has risk aversion. In particular, this conclusion holds both for the linear and log-linear (for $\pi > 0$) demand functions. Furthermore, our numerical examples showed that the monopolistic resource extraction in the first period could be considerably less than what was socially optimal. This was particularly true when the probability of the backstop technology becoming available was high.

CHAPTER 5.

MONOPOLY OF THE RESOURCE WITH AN UNCERTAIN BACKSTOP TECHNOLOGY.

5.1. *The general case.*

We now assume that the resource extracting monopoly does not control the substitute production, if such production becomes possible. When the producers of this substitute are competitive firms, this means that all of the demand will face the monopolist at prices lower than c, and that there will be no demand for the natural resource if a price higher than c is charged and substitute production is possible. It makes no difference for our analysis what we assume about the demand for the border case with $p(t) = c$. In accordance with Hoel (1978 a, b) and Dasgupta and Stiglitz (1976), we shall therefore assume that for $p(t) = c$ the monopolist can sell as much as he wishes up to the total demand following from the demand function in the market.

Like in the case of full monopoly, the resource extracting monopoly will maximize EV* defined by (3.5). If the backstop technology does *not* become feasible, the expression for the discounted profits are of course identical for these two monopoly cases. This means that $V^{II}(x_1)$ is given by (4.3) also in the present case. If the backstop technology *does* become feasible, the discounted profits of the monopolist are given by

$$(5.1) \qquad V^{I}(x_1) = x_1\phi'(x_1) + (1+r)^{-1}[n(x_1)\cdot(S-x_1)],$$

where

$$(5.2) \qquad n(x_1) = \text{Min}[c, \phi'(S-x_1)].$$

Equation (5.1) and (5.2) state that if the backstop technology becomes feasible, the price in the second period will be given by c or $\phi'(S-x_1)$, whichever is lowest. From (5.2) and the fact that $\phi(x_1)$ is strictly concave it is clear that

$$(5.3) \qquad n(x_1) = c \Leftrightarrow x_1 \geqq \tilde{x}_1,$$

where

$$(5.4) \qquad \begin{cases} \tilde{x}_1 = 0 & \text{for } \phi'(S) \geqq c \\ \phi'(S-\tilde{x}_1) = c & \text{for } \phi'(S) < c. \end{cases}$$

Let us look at the case where $\tilde{x}_1$ is positive. Furthermore, imagine that the monopolist should try to choose a value of $x_1 < \tilde{x}_1$. From (3.5), (4.3), (5.1) and (5.2) we then find

$$(5.5) \qquad \frac{\partial(1+r)EV^*}{\partial x_1} = (1+r)[\phi'(x_1)+x_1\phi''(x_1)] - [\phi'(S-x_1)+(S-x_1)\phi''(S-x_1)].$$

Now we know from (1.26) and (1.27) that the expression in (5.5) must be positive for $x_1 < S/2$. But (1.28) together with (5.4) implies that $\tilde{x}_1 < S/2$. This means that a resource extraction lower than $\tilde{x}_1$ cannot be optimal. From (5.3) we therefore know that we must have $n(x_1) = c$ when x_1 is chosen optimally. By inserting this into (5.1) and differentiating (3.5) with (4.3) and (5.1) inserted, we obtain

$$(5.6) \qquad \frac{\partial(1+r)EV^*}{\partial x_1} = (1+r)[\phi'(x_1)+x_1\phi''(x_1)] - \tilde{f}(x_1,\pi),$$

where $\tilde{f}(x_1,\pi)$ is given by (4.7), which we shall repeat for convenience:

$$(5.7) \qquad \tilde{f}(x_1,\pi) = \pi^*c + (1-\pi^*)[\phi'(S-x_1)-(S-x_1)\phi''(S-x_1)].$$

Because of our reasoning above, it is clear that (5.6) only is valid for $x_1 \geqq \tilde{x}_1$, giving the right hand derivative for $x_1 = \tilde{x}_1$ (the left hand derivative for $x_1 = \tilde{x}_1$ is given by (5.5), the reason for $\partial(1+r)EV^*/\partial x_1$ being discontinuous is that $n(x_1)$ is kinked at $x_1 = \tilde{x}_1$).

From our reasoning above it is clear that $\hat{x}_1$ can be found by setting the expression in (5.6) equal to zero. However, if this gives a value lower than $\tilde{x}_1$, then $\tilde{x}_1$ is the optimal solution. Apart from these exceptions, we therefore have $\hat{x}_1$ determined by

$$(5.8) \qquad (1+r)[\phi'(\hat{x}_1) + \hat{x}_1\phi''(\hat{x}_1)] = \tilde{f}(\hat{x}_1,\pi^*).$$

It is clear that this solution is identical to the solution for the case of full monopoly when the latter solution is given by (4.6).[1] From section 4.1 we remember that the solution would be given by (4.6) as long as the monopolist found it profitable to produce some of the substitute, if possible, in the second period. In this case the two monopoly cases therefore give the same development of resource extraction. This may seem surprising, but the reason for this similarity is quite simple to understand: If the backstop technology does *not* become feasible, the profit in period 2 from any given amount of non-extracted resources is of course the same in both monopoly cases, as they become identical in this case. If the backstop technology *does* become feasible, and the monopolist in control of both resource extraction and substitute production finds it profitable to utilize this technology, then the gain to this monopolist in period 2 of a marginal increase of resource extraction in period 2 must be equal to the difference between the cost of producing the substitute and of extracting the resource. But this cost difference is precisely equal to c, which also is the profit in period 2 a monopolist controlling only the resource extraction has from a marginal increase in his resource extraction in period 2. In other words, it is clear that whether or not the backstop technology becomes feasible, the two types of monopoly will have the same increase of profits in period 2 - and of course the same decrease of profits in period 1 - from a marginal decrease of resource extraction in period 1, i.e. a marginal increase of resource extraction in period 2.

---

1) This of course only holds if π^* is the same in both cases, which we shall assume to begin with.

The identity of the two monopoly solutions holds as long as some substitute production is profitable in the case of full monopoly. From section 4.1 we know that when such production is not profitable, the solution was given by (4.5), making the inequality in (4.4) hold. It is easy to demonstrate that in this case our present monopoly case must have a lower resource extraction than we found in the case of full monopoly. This is simplest to show be using a figure similar to figure 4.2, which corresponded to the monopoly solution given by (4.5). Figure 5.1 is identical to figure 4.2, except that we have now also drawn $\tilde{f}(x_1,\pi^*)$. From this figure it is clear that $\hat{x}_1^{rm}$ (rm = resource monopoly), which is the solution to our present monopoly case (unless $\hat{x}_1^{rm} < \tilde{x}$, in which case $\tilde{x}$ is the solution), must be smaller than $\hat{x}_1^{fm}$ (fm = full monopoly), which was the solution in the case of full monopoly. We may also find, like in figure 5.1, that $\hat{x}_1^{rm} < S/2$ in

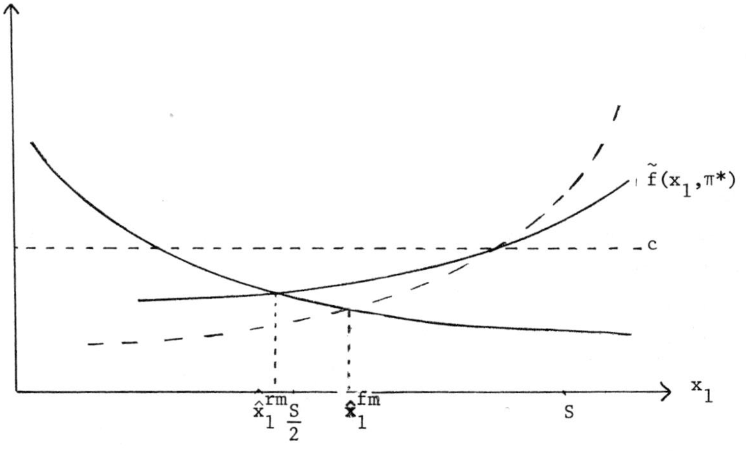

Figure 5.1

the present case, although this does not necessarily occur.

It may seem surpricing that the initial extraction may well be lower - and the initial price higher - in the market structure with a competitively supplied substitute than in the case of full monopoly. This result is derived and interpretet in Hoel (1978b) for the case of certainty, and is also derived in Hoel (1978a, pp. 25-30) for the special case of a linear demand function.

Like in our earlier solutions, we of course find that the resource extraction in period 1 in the present case is larger the larger is S and the larger is r, as long as we do not have any of the two possible corner solutions. Whenever our present solution is identical to the solution in the case of full monopoly, we also must have $\hat{x}_1$ increasing with π^* (this follows from figure 4.1, which covers this case)[1]. However, whenever $\hat{x}_1^{rm} < \hat{x}_1^{fm}$, like in figure 5.1, it follows from this figure that $\hat{x}_1^{rm}$ must be *lower* the higher π^* is (unless we have the corner solution $\hat{x}^{rm} = \tilde{x}$).

By comparing $V^I(\hat{x}_1)$ with $V^{II}(\hat{x}_1)$ (see (5.1) and (4.3)), and using (5.3) and (5.4), it is clear that as long as $\hat{x}_1 > \tilde{x}_1$, we must have $V^I(\hat{x}_1) < V^{II}(\hat{x}_1)$. In other words, the state of the world which is least desirable is the one where the backstop technology does become feasible, so that risk aversion means that $\pi^* > \pi$. From our reasoning above it is therefore clear that risk aversion may give both a higher or a lower level of resource extraction in the first period than one would get with risk neutrality, depending on the circumstances. If $\hat{x}_1 = \tilde{x}_1$, we get $V^I(\tilde{x}_1) = V^{II}(\tilde{x}_1)$ (cf. (4.3), (5.1), (5.3) and (5.4)), so that $\pi^* = \pi$. This means that if the solution is $\tilde{x}$ when there is risk neutrality, this will also be the solution if there is risk aversion, and vica versa.

The relationship between the two monopoly cases when there is risk aversion in both cases is as follows: If the resource extraction in the two cases is identical when there is risk neutrality, then risk aversion will imply that the extraction in period 1 when the monopolist only controls the resource extraction ($\hat{x}_1^{rm}$) is higher than the extraction in period 1 in the case of full monopoly ($\hat{x}_1^{rf}$). On the other hand, if $\hat{x}_1^{rm} < \hat{x}_1^{rf}$ when there is risk neutrality, this difference will be even larger when there is risk aversion.

The present case resembles the competitive case in the sense that in both cases risk aversion gives us $\pi^* > \pi$, while risk aversion implied $\pi^* < \pi$ in the case of full monopoly. However, in the competitive case a consequence of this was that the resource extraction in period 1 was higher with risk coversion than it was with risk neutrality. We have just seen that this consequence does not necessarily follow from $\pi^* > \pi$ in the present case.

---

1) In the special case where all three lines in figure 4.2 intersect in one point, we get $\hat{x}_1^{rm} = \hat{x}_1^{rf}$, and this resource extraction is not influences by the value of π^*.

For a sufficiently low value of c we can never get a solution like the one following from figure 5.1. This means that for a sufficiently low value of c the resource extraction in period 1 in the present case will always be higher with risk aversion than it would be with risk neutrality.

Like in the monopoly case treated in chapter 4, it is not obvious that the present monopoly case will have a lower resource extraction in period 1 than what is socially optimal. For $\pi = \pi^*$ in both cases, however, we have just seen that the present monopoly case never will have a higher initial resource extraction than the case of full monopoly. Together with a result derived in section 4.1 (pp. 48-50), we therefore can conclude that a sufficient condition for the present monopoly case to have less initial extraction than what is socially optimal is that the demand elasticity is higher the higher the price is and the monopolist is risk neutral.

Even if the resource extraction was higher than the socially optimal level in the case of full monopoly when $\pi^* = \pi$, the existence of risk aversion in the case of full monopoly would tend to make the extraction lower than what was socially optimal. In the present monopoly case, however, the existence of risk aversion may draw in the opposite direction. This means that one may well find that the resource extracting monopoly will extract more than what is socially optimal in the first period.

5.2. Linear demand function.

Assume now that the demand function is given by (2.8). To begin with, let us find $\tilde{x}_1$ in this case. From (5.4) we obtain

$$(5.9)\quad \begin{cases} \tilde{x}_1 = 0 & \text{for} \quad a-bS \geqq c \\ \tilde{x}_1 = S - \frac{a-c}{b} & \text{for} \quad a-bS < c\,. \end{cases}$$

Unless the optimal resource extraction in the present case is equal to $\tilde{x}_1$ or S, it must be given by (5.8), which in the present case may be written

$$(5.10)\qquad \hat{x}_1 = \frac{ra + \pi^*(a-c) + (1-\pi^*)2bS}{(2+r-\pi^*)2b}\,.$$

In section 4.2 we saw that a linear demand function implied that the demand elasticity $\eta(x_1)$ decreased with x_1. From our general discussion in section 5.1 (p. 63) we can therefore conclude that as long as the resource extracting monopolist is risk neutral, its resource extraction in the first period is lower than what is socially optimal.[1] However, if the monopolist has a sufficiently high degree of risk aversion we might well get the opposite conclusion, i.e. too much resource extraction in the monopoly case.

In Hoel (1978a, pp. 25-30) have showed that the present monopoly case with a linear demand function *always* would give a lower initial resource extraction than the competitive case (equal to the social optimum) when the backstop technology was feasible from the start. Our present analysis of this monopoly case shows that this conclusion also holds even if the backstop technology does not become feasible before the second period, as long as it is known with certainty that it will become feasible (i.e. π=1). However, when the availability of the backstop technology is uncertain (i.e. $0 < \pi < 1$), we mentioned that the present monopoly case *may* have a

---

[1] This holds for $r > 0$, for r=0 the two solutions are identical if $\pi = \pi^* = 0$.

higher resource extraction that what is socially optimal. The numerical example which follows will demonstrate this possibility.

We now turn to our numerical example, with our parameters given by (2.11) and (2.12), i.e. c = 1,75. It follows from (5.9) that in this case we get $\tilde{x}_1 = 9{,}64$. Remembering this lower boundary for $\hat{x}_1$, we find $\hat{x}_1$ from (5.10), see table 5.1

Resource extraction ($\hat{x}_1$) with a resource extracting monopolist when c = 1,75 (linear demand function given by (2.7) and (2.12)).

π^* \ r	0,5	0
0	51,3	50,0
0,25	50,9	49,3
0,5	50,4	48,4
0,75	49,8	47,1
1	48,9	45,2

Table 5.1

From table 5.1 we see that $\hat{x}_1$ in the present case decreases with π^*, although this affect is quite weak. In the case where the monopoly had control also over the backstop technology, we found that $\hat{x}_1$ was independent of π^*, equal to 51,3 and 50,0 for r=0,5 and r=0, respectively. The results in table 5.1 are quite close to these values. Like in the other monopoly case, we see that the results in table 5.1 imply that the resource extraction in the first period is considerably lower than what is socially optimal (see table 2.1).

Let us now instead of c = 1,75 look at the case where c = 0,1. From (5.9) we see that in this case $\tilde{x}_1 = 0$. The results for $\hat{x}_1$ follow from (5.10), and are identical to the results found in the case of full monopoly, given by table 4.1. We see that $\hat{x}_1$ now increases with increasing π^*, although this effect is quite weak. When r = 0.5 , we see that $\hat{x}_1$ for $\pi^*=1$ in table 4.1 is lower than $\hat{x}_1$ for $\pi=0$ in table 2.2. This means that for r=0,5 the monopolist will extract less in period 1 than what is socially optimal no matter how large a degree of risk aversion he has. For r=0 one can get the opposite result if π is sufficiently close to zero, but this would require an extremely high degree of risk aversion.

5.3. *Log-linear demand function.*

When the demand function is given by (2.14), we see from (5.4) that $\tilde{x}_1$ is given by

$$(5.11) \quad \begin{cases} \tilde{x}_1 = 0 & \text{for} \quad AS^{-\beta} \geqq c \\ A(S-\tilde{x}_1)^{-\beta} = c & \text{for} \quad AS^{-\beta} < c\,. \end{cases}$$

Unless the optimal resource extraction in the present case is equal to $\tilde{x}_1$ or S, it must be given by (5.8), which in the present case may be written

$$(5.12) \quad (1+r)\hat{x}_1^{\,-\beta} = \pi^*\frac{c}{(1-\beta)A} + (1-\pi^*)(S-\hat{x}_1)^{-\beta} .$$

Like in the monopoly case treated in section (4.3), it is clear from (5.12) that $\hat{x}_1$ = S only can be a solution if π^*=1.

If there is no chance of a backstop technology becoming feasible (i.e. $\pi^* = \pi = 0$), our present monopoly case is of course identical to the monopoly case treated in chapter 4. In this case we saw (p. 55) that when the demand function was log-linear this monopoly case had a resource extraction identical to what was socially optimal and was the competitive solution.

Let us now assume that π is positive, and that we have risk neutrality, i.e. $\pi^* = \pi$. In section 4.3 (p. 55) we saw that the monopoly case treated there always would have less resource extraction than what was socially optimal as long as $\pi^* = \pi$ was positive. Furthermore, in our general treatment of our present monopoly case in section 5.1 we found that the present monopoly case never could have a higher resource extraction in the first period than the case of full monopoly had as long as π^* was the same in both cases. We can therefore conclude that as long as risk aversion is disregarded, the present monopoly case will have a lower resource extraction than what is socially optimal when π is positive.

In the case of risk aversion we have $\pi^* > \pi$ in our present monopoly case. We have seen that this *may* imply a larger resource extraction in the first period than we would have got with risk neutrality. This effect *may* be stronger than the effect of our monopoly case having a lower initial resource extraction than what is socially optimal. In other words, there is a possibility of our present monopoly case having a higher resource extraction in the first period than what is socially optimal.

We now turn to our numerical example, with our parameters given by (2.12) and (2.17), i.e. c = 1,75. It follows from (5.11) that in this case we get $\tilde{x}_1 = 46{,}2$. Taking this lower boundary for $\hat{x}_1$ into consideration (5.12) gives us the results for $\hat{x}_1$, see table 5.2.

Resource extraction ($\hat{x}_1$) with a resource extracting monopolist when c = 1,75 (log-linear demand function given by (2.11) and (2.17)).

π^* \ r	0,5	0
0	61,0	50,0
0,25	46,2	46,2
0,5	46,2	46,2
0,75	46,2	46,2
1	46,2	46,2

Table 5.2

In the case of full monopoly we found that $\hat{x}_1$ was independent of π^*, equal to 61,0 and 50,0 for r=0,5 and r=0, respectively. In our present case $\hat{x}_1$ falls rapidly from these values as π^* increases above zero, and quickly reaches it's lower boundary 46,2. Comparing table 5.2 with table 2.3, we see that our monopolist will extract considerably less of the resource in the first period than what is socially optimal for any values of π not too close to zero.

Let us now instead of c = 1,75 look at the case where c = 0,1. From (5.11) we see that in this case $\tilde{x}_1 = 0$. The results for $\hat{x}_1$ follow from (5.12), and are identical to the results found in the case of full monopoly, given by table 4.2. In other words, in this case $\hat{x}_1$ increases quite significantly with increasing values of π^*. Comparing with table 2.4 we see that if our present monopolist has risk aversion we may find that our monopolist extracts *more* of the resource in period 1 that what is socially optimal. For instance, if π=0,25 and the monopolist's risk aversion implies that π^*=0,75, the monopolist extracts 79,9% of the total resource deposit in the first period, while it is optimal to extract only 68,0%.

5.4. Summary of chapter 5.

When risk aversion was disregarded, we found that the initial resource extraction of a monopolist *not* controlling the backstop technology was equal to or lower than what it would be for a monopolist controlling the backstop technology as well as the resource extraction. Unlike any of the market structures treated earlier, the present monopoly case could have a solution where the resource extraction increased - and resource price declined even if the backstop technology did not become available - over time.

In the present monopoly case there was no unambiguous answer to the question about in which direction initial resource extraction changed when the probability of substitute production becoming technically feasible increased. Similarly, risk aversion could imply both a lower and a higher initial resource extraction than what one would find with risk neutrality. Comparing the two monopoly cases, we found that if the initial resource extraction was equal in the two cases when there was risk neutrality, the monopoly case treated in the present chapter would have the highest resource extraction in period 1 in the case of risk aversion. On the other hand, if the monopoly case treated in the present chapter had a lower initial resource extraction than one found in the case of full monopoly when there was risk neutrality, this relationship between the two monopoly cases would be the same also in the case with risk aversion.

Like for the monopoly case treated in chapter 4, we cannot be sure that the present monopoly case always will have a lower initial resource extraction than what is socially optimal. However, as long as risk aversion is disregarded, this will be the case for most reasonable specifications of the demand function. In particular, this conclusion holds both for linear and log-linear (for $\pi > 0$) demand functions. On the other hand, when the monopolist has risk aversion we may well find that the initial resource extraction is higher than socially optimal, even for reasonable demand functions. Our numerical examples showed that this could occur both with the linear and the log-linear demand function when the probability of the backstop technology becoming feasible was not too high. However, the general tendency observed from the numerical examples was that the monopolist's resource extraction in the first period usually was lower - sometimes considerably lower - than what was socially optimal. Both the direction and the magnitude of the difference between the monopolist's extraction and the socially optimal extraction depended on the specification of the demand function, the cost of producing the substitute, the discount rate, the probability of such production becoming feasible and on the degree of risk aversion assumed.

CHAPTER 6.
SOCIALLY OPTIMAL AND COMPETITIVE RESOURCE EXTRACTION WITH AN UNCERTAIN RESOURCE STOCK.

6.1. Introduction.

In the following chapters we shall assume that it is known with certainty that the backstop technology will be feasible in period 2, although it is not feasible in period 1. However, we shall now assume that the actual magnitude of the initial resource stock, S, is not known with certainty. More precisely, we assume that a stock S* is known with certainty, and is available for period 1 and 2. In period 1, exploration takes place (exogeneously in our analysis, cf. p. 4), and the results of this exploration will be known before the decision about how much of the substitute is to be produced in period 2 is made. In the beginning of period 1, however, the result of exploration is not known with certainty. We shall assume that there exists a discrete probability distribution, agreed upon by all relevant agents in the economy, for the results of the exploration. The lowest value of this distribution is assumed to be zero, and the maximal and mean value are denoted by $S^{**}-S^*$ and $\bar{S}-S^*$, respectively. In general we shall assume there are n possible outcomes, $\bar{S}+q_1-S^*,\ldots,\bar{S}+q_n-S^*$, where the probability of q_i is $\pi_i > 0$. The properties of our distribution may be summarized by

$$
(6.1)\quad \begin{cases} \Sigma_i \pi_i = 1 , & \Sigma_i \pi_i q_i = 0, \\ \underset{i}{\mathrm{Min}}[q_i] = -(\bar{S}-S^*), & \underset{i}{\mathrm{Max}}[q_i] = S^{**}-\bar{S}. \end{cases}
$$

Looked upon from the beginning of period 1, the total stock S is given by a probability distribution with $\bar{S}$ as the mean value, and S* and S** as the smallest and largest possible values, respectively.

In part of our reasoning we shall simplify the analysis considerably, by assuming that the exploration will give no result with probability π, and give an additional stock $S^{**}-S^*$ with the probability $1-\pi$. This can be simplified further by assuming $\pi=1/2$, so that $\bar{S} = (S^{**} - S^*)/2$ and $-q_1 = q_2 = q = \bar{S} - S^* = S^{**} - \bar{S}$.

In section 1.4 we made some assumptions which implied that the resource was scarce and that it was socially desireable to use the backstop technology in the second period (cf. (1.27)-(1.28)). If we simply substitute S by $\bar{S}$ in these formulas, it might well turn out that the exploration gives such a high value of S-S* that not all of the resource is used in period 2, and that it is socially optimal not to use the backstop technology. This will be the case if only slightly more than S*/2 is used in period 1, the exploration gives the highest possible value of new resources, and $\phi'(S^{**} - S^*/2)$ is considerably below c_1. To avoid such situations, we shall assume that

$$(6.2) \qquad \phi'(S^{**} - \frac{S^*}{2}) + (S^{**} - \frac{S^*}{2})\phi''(S^{**} - \frac{S^*}{2}) > c_1,$$

which means that even if as much new resources as possible are found through exploration, and only S*/2 is used in period 1, a monopolist will use all the remaining resources in period 2. This inequality also implies

$$(6.2') \qquad \phi'(S^{**} - \frac{S^*}{2}) > c_1,$$

so that it will always be socially optimal to use all the reamining resource stock in period 2. Furthermore, we shall assume that

$$(6.3) \qquad \phi'(S^{**} - \frac{S^*}{2}) > c_2,$$

so that it always will be socially optimal to use the backstop technology in period 2.

The assumptions (6.2) and (6.3) correspond to our assumptions (1.27) and (1.28) when S was known with certainty. Like before, we shall assume that (1.29) holds, i.e. $c_1=0$. The simplified notation $c_2=c$ will also be used.

Before finding the social optimum, one point should be made. We have implicitly assumed that the resource extraction in the first period cannot exceed S*. This is reasonable with the interpretation of the uncertainty given above, i.e. that it is the results from some exploration activity which are uncertain. Alternatively, we could have assumed that no exploration was being done, but that the information relevant for estimating the remaining stock gradually improves as extraction takes place (cf. the discussion in section 1.2). In our simple two-period model this would mean that we could not disregard the possibility of the resource extraction exceeding S* in the first period, if the actual S turned out to be larger than S*. When this is allowed for, the desicion in the beginning of period 1 will be planned extraction instead of actual extraction, the two only being equal if it turns out that the actual resource stock is not smaller than the planned extraction. In the real world, information about the true size of the resource stock will be reveiled partly by exploration, and partly by the process of extracting the resource. However, we shall stick to our interpretation about the uncertainty arizing only from uncertain results of exploration, so that the constraint $x_1 \leqq S^*$ can be justified.

6.2. *Socially optimal resource extraction.*

Like before, we assume that the social objective function is given by (2.1), which we shall repeat for convenience:

$$(6.4) \qquad Z = \phi(x_1) + (1+r)^{-1}[\phi(S-x_1+x_2) - cx_2].$$

Whatever value for x_1 one has chosen for period 1, x_2 must be given by a rule depending on the information in the beginning of period 2:

$$(6.5) \qquad x_2 = \hat{x}_2(x_1,S).$$

Note that S enters the function determining x_2, because the true size of S is known when the decision about x_2 is made. The function $\hat{x}_2(x_1,S)$

defines the value of x_2 which maximizes Z for whatever value of x_1 one has chosen and whatever the true size of the resource stock turns out to be. From (6.4) it is clear that $\hat{x}_2(x_1,S)$ must be given by

$$(6.6) \qquad \phi'(S - x_1 + \hat{x}_2(x_1,S)) = c.$$

We have disregarded the possibility of $\hat{x}_2(x_1,S) = 0$, as this can only be optimal if $\phi'(S-x_1) \leqq c$. From (6.3) it is clear that whichever of the values in the interval $[S^*,S^{**}]$ turns out to be the true value of S, $\phi'(S-x_1) \leqq c$ can only occur if $x_1 < S^*/2$. As we soon shall see, the optimal value of x_1 will never be so small.

In the beginning of period 1 the decision-maker does not know the true size of the resource stock. The value of Z will therefore be uncertain for any given value of x_1. Like before, the choice is therefore made by maximizing the expected value of Z. Maximizing EZ is of course the same as maximizing (1+r)EZ, which is given by the following expression:

$$(6.7) \qquad (1+r)EZ = (1+r)\phi(x_1) + \Sigma_i\ \pi_i[\phi(\bar{S} + q_i - x_1 + \hat{x}_2(x_1,\ \bar{S}+q_i)) - c\hat{x}_2(x_1,\ \bar{S}+q_i)],$$

where we have inserted $S = \bar{S}+q_i$. This is a concave function in x_1, it is therefore clear that $\hat{x}_1$ maximizes (1+r)EZ if and only if $\partial(1+r)EZ(\hat{x}_1)/\partial x_1 = 0$, disregarding at first possible corner solutions. Differentiating (6.7) and using (6.1) and (6.6) therefore gives the following formula determining $\hat{x}_1$:

$$(6.8) \qquad \phi'(\hat{x}_1) = (1+r)^{-1}c.$$

In other words, $\hat{x}_1$ is independent not only of the probability distribution of the uncertain stock, but also of the expected value of the resource stock. Before interpreting this result, let us investigate the possibilities of the corner solutions $\hat{x}_1 = 0$ and $\hat{x}_1 = S^*$.

The solution given by (6.8) must always satisfy $\hat{x}_1 > S^{**} - S^*/2 > S^*/2$ because of (6.3) and $r \geqq 0$. This means that the corner solution $\hat{x}_1 = 0$ can be disregarded. However, for a sufficiently high value of r and/or low value of c, the value of $\hat{x}_1$ following from (6.8) may well exceed S*. In this case (6.8) is not valid, and we instead get the corner solution $\hat{x}_1 = S^*$. Like before, corner solutions will be disregarded in the following analysis, except of course whenever they occur in numerical examples.

It may seem surpricing that the optimal resource extraction in the first period is independent of the probability distribution and mean value of the resource stock. The reason for this result is that our assumption (6.3) implies that whatever the true size of the initial resource stock turns out to be, it is optimal to have a positive production of the substitute in the second period. The optimal level of substitute production is determined by (6.6), which states that the sum of the resource extraction and substitute production in period two is determined independent of x_1 and S. But since this sum is independent of S, the true size of S only affects the total cost of supplying this sum of the resource and the substitute. This cost will enter the objective function Z as a linear term independent of x_1. Because of this, the optimal resource extraction in the first period will be independent of this cost term, and therefore independent of the probability distribution and mean value of the initial resource stock.

The optimal resource extraction in the first period will only depend on the discount factor and the cost of producing the substitute. From (6.8) it is clear that the initial resource extraction is higher the higher is the discount factor and the lower is the cost of producing the substitute.

It is easy to see that if we instead of maximizing EZ maximized the expected value of any strictly increasing function of Z, our results would not be changed. In other words, even if the central planning agency has risk aversion, the optimal resource extraction will be independent of the probability distribution and mean value of the resource stock.

6.3. The competitive solution.

The general considerations given in section 3.1 are valid also in the present case, except that we now have more than two states of the world. In particular, it is straightforward to show that risk aversion can be taken care of by substituting all the probabilities π_i with π_i^*, such that $\pi_i^* > \pi_i$ for all i giving a value $\bar{S}+q_i$ considered less desirable by the firm than $\bar{S}$, and $\pi_i^* < \pi_i$ for all i giving a value $\bar{S}+q_i$ considered more desirable by the firm than $\bar{S}$. Of course, the explicit values π_i^* cannot be known before one knows the optimal solution, but the signs of all $\pi_i^*-\pi_i$ are known before the optimal solution is derived.

Like we had in section 3.2 (cf. (3.8)), the competitive resource extracting firm will maximize

$$EV^* = p(1)x_1 + (1+r)^{-1}\Sigma_i\, \pi_i^*[p_i(2)(\bar{S} + q_i - x_1)], \tag{6.9}$$

where p(1) and $p_i(2)$ are the prices of the resource in period 1 and 2, respectively. Unless we have a corner solution (i.e. $x_1 = 0$ or $x_1 = S^*$), we therefore must have

$$\Sigma_i\, \pi_i^* p_i(2) = (1+r)p(1). \tag{6.10}$$

Like before, the equilibrium price in period 1 is determined by

$$p(1) = \phi'(x_1). \tag{6.11}$$

The equilibrium price in period 2 can obviously not exceed c. If $p_i(2) < c$ for some i, we must have $p_i(2) = \phi'(\bar{S} + q_i - x_1) < c$ for these i, which would imply $\phi'(S^{**} - x_1) < c$. But because of (6.3) this could only be true if $x_1 < S^*/2$. However, it is easy to see that $p_i(2) \leq c$ for all i together with (6.3), (6.10) and (6.11) implies that $x_1 > S^*/2$. In other words, we must have $p_i(2) = c$ no matter what the true size of the resource stock turns out to be. Together with (6.11) this gives us (6.8), i.e. the competitive resource extraction will always be socially optimal. This holds no matter what the probabibility distribution and mean value of the resource stock is (as long as (6.3) holds), and independent of whether or not the competitive resource extracting firms have risk aversion.[1)]

The price development follows from (6.8) and (6.11):

$$(6.12) \qquad p(2) = (1+r)p(1),$$

i.e. the price increases with a rate equal to the discount factor. This holds as long as $\hat{x}_1 < S^*$, if the corner solution $\hat{x}_1 = S^*$ occurs, the price may rise with a rate lower than the discount factor, or even decline.

---

1) It is easy to see that this also holds for the corner solution $\hat{x}_1 = S^*$. The solution $\hat{x}_1 = 0$ cannot occur either for the optimal or competitive solution.

6.4. Linear and log-linear demand functions.

With our linear demand function (2.7) we have

$$(6.13) \qquad \phi'(x) = a - bx ,$$

and the optimal initial resource extraction follows from (6.8):

$$(6.14) \qquad \hat{x}_1 = \frac{a - (1+r)^{-1}c}{b} .$$

Similarly, with the log-linear demand function (2.13) we have

$$(6.15) \qquad \phi'(x) = Ax^{-\beta},$$

and the optimal initial resource extraction is

$$(6.16) \qquad \hat{x}_1 = \left(\frac{c}{(1+r)A}\right)^{-\frac{1}{\beta}} .$$

Let us consider a simple numerical example. Like before, we shall let the coefficients in the demand functions be given by (2.12) and (2.17). We shall look at the solutions for r=0,5 and r=0, but only consider the case where c=1,75. As for the distribution of S, it would seem natural to consider a distribution with a mean value equal to 100, which was the value S was assumed to have in chapters 2-5. However, it is easy to see that if $\bar{S}$ = 100, S** - S* must be quite small for (6.2) and (6.3) to be satisfied. To allow for a larger degree of uncertainty we shall therefore let

$$
(6.17)\quad \begin{cases} S = S^* = 40 & \text{with probability} \quad \pi = 1/2 \\ S = S^{**} = 70 & \text{" \qquad "} \quad 1-\pi = 1/2, \end{cases}
$$

giving $\bar{S} = 55$. It is easy to verify that (2.12), (2.17), (6.17) and c=1,75 satisfy our requirements (6.2) and (6.3).

With the linear demand function (given by (6.13) and (2.12)) equation (6.14) gives $\hat{x}_1 = 97{,}9$ for r=0,5 and $\hat{x}_1 = 90{,}4$ for r=0. In other words, the corner solution $\hat{x}_1 = S^* = 40$ will be valid in the present case. If $S = \bar{S} = 55$ with certainty, our solution would be $\hat{x}_1 = 55$.

With the log-linear demand function (given by (6.15) and (2.17)) equation (6.16) gives $\hat{x}_1 = 84{,}3$ for r=0,5 and $\hat{x}_1 = 53{,}8$ for r=0. In other words, the corner solution $\hat{x}_1 = S^* = 40$ is valid also in this case. In the case of $S = \bar{S} = 55$ with certainty, our solution would be $\hat{x}_1 = 55$ for r=0,5 and $\hat{x}_1 = 53{,}8$ for r=0.

6.5. *Summary of chapter 6.*

With the assumptions used, we have shown that the competitive solution is socially optimal irrespectively of whether or not the resource extracting firms or society as a whole has risk aversion. This competitive and optimal solution will have a resource extraction in the first period which either is independent of all properties of the probability distribution of the size of the resource stock, or is equal to the total stock available for extraction in the first period.

For both numerical specifications of demand functions studied, we found that the competitive and optimal solutions implied extracting as much as possible in the first period when the probability distribution of the uncertain stock was given by (6.17).

CHAPTER 7.
FULL MONOPOLY WITH AN UNCERTAIN RESOURCE STOCK.

7.1. The general case.

Like before, we assume that the monopolist maximizes

$$(7.1) \qquad EV^*(x_1,S) = x_1\phi'(x_1) + (1+r)^{-1}EV_2^*(x_1,S).$$

where $V_2(x_1,S)$ is the maximized profit in period 2 given that x_1 is extracted in period 1 and that the true initial resource stock turns out to be S. More precisely,

$$(7.2) \qquad V_2(x_1,S) = \underset{x_2 \geq 0}{\text{Max}}[(S-x_1+x_2)\phi'(S-x_1+x_2)-cx_2]$$

and

$$(7.3) \qquad EV_2^*(x_1,S) = \Sigma_i\pi^*_iV_2(x_1,\bar{S}+q_1).$$

Like before, the true values of π^*_i can only be known after the optimal x_1 is found (cf. p. 75). However, we know that $\pi^*_i = \pi_i$ if the monopolist is risk neutral, and $\pi^*_i > \pi_i$ or $\pi^*_i < \pi_i$ depending on whether $\bar{S} + q_i$ is considered less or more desirable for the monopolist than $\bar{S}$ if the monopolist has risk aversion. Obviously, the monopolist considers the outcomes with the highest resource stocks as the most desirable, so that we must have $(\pi^*_i-\pi_i)q_i \leqq 0$, where a strict inequality holds when $q_i \neq 0$ and the monopolist is risk averse.

The monopolist's optimal resource extraction in period 1, $\hat{x}_1$, is given by $\delta EV^*/\delta x_1 = 0$ (disregarding the possibilities of $\hat{x}_1 = S$). By using (7.1) and (7.2) we therefore obtain

$$(7.4)\qquad \phi'(\hat{x}_1) + \hat{x}_1\phi''(\hat{x}_1) = -(1+r)^{-1}\Sigma_i\pi^*_i \frac{\delta V_2(\hat{x}_1,\bar{S}+q_i)}{\delta x_1}.$$

Because of the concavity of $x\phi'(x)$, the function $V_2(x_1,S)$ may be written as

$$V_2(x_1,S) = (S-x_1+\hat{x}_2(x_1,S))\phi'(S-x_1+\hat{x}_2(x_1,S)) - c\hat{x}_2(x_1,S),$$

where $\hat{x}_2(x_1,S)$ is non-negative and satisfies

$$\phi'(S-x_1+\hat{x}_2(x_1,S)) + (S-x_1+\hat{x}_2(x_1,S))\phi''(S-x_1+\hat{x}_2(x_1,S)) \leqq c,$$

where the equation sign holds for $\hat{x}_2(x_1,S)$ positive. Using this way of expressing $V_2(x_1,S)$, it is easy to show that

$$(7.5)\qquad -\frac{\delta V_2(x_1,S)}{\delta x_1} = \begin{cases} c \text{ for } \phi'(S-x_1) + (S-x_1)\phi''(S-x_1) \geqq c, \\ \phi'(S-x_1) + (S-x_1)\phi''(S-x_1) \\ \text{for } \phi'(S-x_1) + (S-x_1)\phi''(S-x_1) \leqq c. \end{cases}$$

Together with (7.4) we therefore have

$$(7.6)\qquad \phi'(\hat{x}_1) + \hat{x}_1\phi''(\hat{x}_1) \leqq (1+r)^{-1}c .$$

Let us look closer at some special cases. First, assume that whatever q_i turns out to be, it will be optimal to have positive substitute production in period 2. In other words, we are assuming that $\hat{x}_2(\hat{x}_1,\bar{S}+q_i) > 0$ for all i, which will hold if and only if

$$\phi'(\bar{S}+q_i-\hat{x}_1) + (\bar{S}+q_i-\hat{x}_1)\phi''(\bar{S}+q_i-\hat{x}_1) \geqq c$$

for all q_i. Since $x\phi'(x)$ is concave and $S^{**} \geqq \bar{S} + q_i$ for all i, this is equivailent to the assumption that

$$\phi'(S^{**}-\hat{x}_1) + (S^{**}-\hat{x}_1)\phi''(S^{**}-\hat{x}_1) \geqq c \tag{7.7}$$

To summarize, we have shown that (7.6) will hold with equality if and only if S** is so small that (7.7) holds.

Before leaving the case where (7.6) holds with equality, let us comapre this solution with the social optimum and the competitive case. Because of assumption (6.3), the social optimum would have a positive substitute production in period 2 no matter what the true size of the resource stock turns out to be. However, (6.3) is not sufficient to guarantee that the monopolist will produce the substitute in period 2. If (7.7) holds, however, the monopolist will produce the substitute in period 2 no matter what the true size of the resource stock turns out to be. In this case the solution of the monopolist is very similar to the socially optimal solution: Both solutions are independent of the probability distribution and the expected value of the uncertain stock, and of whether or not the decision-maker has risk aversion. The difference between the two solutions is that while in the competitive and optimal solution the resource price in period 1 was equal to the discounted unit cost of producing the substitute, it is the marginal revenue from extracting the resource in period 1 which equals this discounted unit cost in the case of monopoly. A consequence of this difference is that the initial resource extraction in the monopoly case is lower than what is socially optimal.

We shall now turn to the case which is in a sense the opposite of what we just have looked at: Assume that whatever q_i turns out to be, it will be optimal for the monopolist *not* to have any substitute production in period 2. In other words, we are assuming that $\hat{x}_2(\hat{x}_1,\bar{S}+q_i) = 0$ for all i, which will hold if and only if

$$(7.8) \qquad \phi'(S^*-\hat{x}_1) + (S^*-\hat{x}_1)\phi''(S^*-\hat{x}_1) \leqq c,$$

where we have used $S^* \leqq \bar{S} + q_i$ for all i and the fact that $x\phi'(x)$ is concave. In other words, the solution $\hat{x}_1$ is given by (cf. (7.4) and (7.5))

$$(7.9) \qquad \phi'(\hat{x}_1) + \hat{x}_1\phi''(\hat{x}_1) = (1+r)^{-1}\Sigma_i\pi^*_i\,[\phi'(S+q_i-\hat{x}_1) + (S+q_i-\hat{x}_1)\phi''(S+q_i-\hat{x}_1)]$$

if and only if (7.8) holds when $\hat{x}_1$ is inserted from (7.9) into (7.8). Let us compare the solution given by (7.9) with the corresponding solution with a certain resource stock, i.e. when $q_i = 0$ is the only possible outcome for q_i. The term in brackets in (7.9) is the marginal revenue in period 2, which we have assumed is a decreasing function of the output of that period. If $\phi'(x) + x\phi''(x)$ in addition to being decreasing in x also is strictly convex in x, we must have, assuming risk neutrality at first,

$$(7.10) \qquad \Sigma_i\pi_i[\phi'(\bar{S}+q_i-x_1) + (\bar{S}+q_i-x_1)\phi''(\bar{S}+q_i-x_1)] >$$
$$\phi'(\bar{S}-x_1) + (\bar{S}-x_1)\phi''(\bar{S}-x_1).$$

If we have risk neutrality, i.e. $\pi^*_i = \pi_i$, it is clear that (7.9) and (7.10) taken together imply that $\hat{x}_1$ must be lower in the case with uncertainty than in the case where the resource stock is known with certainty. If the marginal revenue function $\phi'(x) + x\phi''(x)$ is strictly concave, the inequality sign is reversed, so that the initial resource extraction in this case is higher when there is uncertainty than when the resource stock is known with certainty. In the special case where $\phi'(x) + x\phi''(x)$ is linear, the uncertainty does not affect the initial resource extraction as long as there is no risk aversion. The sign of the second order derivative of $\phi'(x)+\phi''(x)$ may of course depend on x, in this case we cannot draw any general conclusion about in which direction uncertainty will tend to move the monopolist's optimal resource extraction. Before proceding, we shall illustrate how uncertainty affects the resource extraction in period 1 in the simple case when $-q_1 = q_2 = q = \bar{S}-S^*$ and $\pi_1=\pi_2=\frac{1}{2}$. In figure 7.1 the downward sloping curve m is the graph of $(1+r)(\phi'(x_1)+x_1\phi_1''(x_1))$, and the two non-vertical dotted curve 1* and 1** are the graphs of $\phi'(S^*-x_1)+(S^*-x_1)\phi''(S^*-x_1)$ and $\phi'(S^{**}-x_1)+(S^{**}-x_1)\phi''(S^{**}-x_1)$, respectively. In this figure we have assumed that the marginal revenue function is strictly convex everywhere. The curve l is equally distanced from l^* and l^{**}, measured *vertically*. On the other hand, the curve $\bar{l}$ is equally distanced from l^* and l^{**}, measured *horizontally*. Obviously, l must lie to the left of $\bar{l}$ when the curves l^* and l^{**} are strictly convex. From (7.9) we see that $\hat{x}_1$ must be the value of x_1 which makes

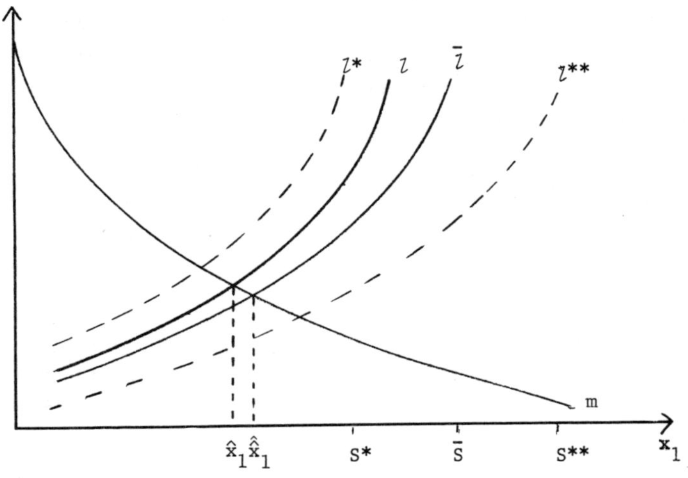

Figure 7.1

m intersect with l. Furthermore, in the case of certainty the optimal x_1, denoted by $\hat{\hat{x}}_1$, must be the value of x_1 which makes m intersect with $\bar{l}$. From the figure we see that $\hat{x}_1 < \hat{\hat{x}}_1$. If the curves l^* and l^{**} had been concave, l would have been to the right of $\bar{l}$, so that in this case we would find $\hat{x}_1 > \hat{\hat{x}}_1$. In the special case where the curves l^* and l^{**} are straight lines, l and $\bar{l}$ would be identical, so that $\hat{x}_1 = \hat{\hat{x}}_1$.

So far we have compared the case where the resource stock is uncertain with the case of full certainty. Another question one could ask is how $\hat{x}_1$ would be affected by a small increase in the degree of uncertainty. Let us look at this question for the special case illustrated in figure 7.1. An increase in q (i.e. moving S* to the left and S** to the right) will leave the mean value $\bar{S}$ unchanged but increase the variance of our probability distribution. From figure (7.1) it is easy to see that an increase in q will move l upwards, downwards or leave l unchanged depending on whether the marginal revenue function is strictly convex, strictly concave or linear. In other words, how an increased uncertainty will effect the monopolist's resource extraction in period l will depend on the curvature of its marginal revenue function.

Let us now turn to the case with risk aversion, and compare this with the case where the probability distribution of S is the same, but where the monopolist is risk neutral. We mentioned earlier (cf. p. 215) that $(\pi^*_i - \pi_i)q_i < 0$ for $q_i \neq 0$ when we have risk avresion. Furthermore, the term in brackets in (7.9) is higher, cet.par., the lower is q_i. Starting from $\pi_i = \pi^*_i$ in (7.9) and increasing (decreasing) π^*_i for $q_i < 0$ ($q_i > 0$) therefore increases the weighs of the higher terms on the right hand side of (7.9) compared with the weights of the lower terms. For an unchanged $\hat{x}_1$, the right hand side of (7.9) will therefore increase. To preserve the equation, $\hat{x}_1$ must therefore decrease when we move from a situation with risk neutrality to a situation with risk aversion. In other words, the monopolist's optimal extraction in period 1 is lower if he has risk aversion than if he is risk neutral. This conclusion holds no matter how the curvature of the marginal revenue function is, as long as our solution is given by (7.9). If the marginal revenue function is convex, this result together with our earlier results implies that the monopolist's initial extraction always will be lower when the resource stock is uncertain than when the resource stock is known with certainty. On the other hand, if the marginal revenue function is concave, the degree of risk aversion will determine whether or not the initial resource extraction will be lower in the case of uncertainty than in the case of certainty.

In our simple case illustrated by figure 7.1, risk aversion means that the line l should lie closer to l^* than to l^{**} (measured vertically). In other words, introducing risk aversion shifts l upwards, which of course decreases $\hat{\hat{x}}_1$.

Let us now turn to the cases where the monopolist's decision whether or not to produce the substitute in period 2 depends on what the true size of the resource stock turns out to be. In other words, which of the two expressions for $\delta V_2(x_1,S)/\delta x_1$ in (7.5) will be valid will depend on which $S \in [S^*,S^{**}]$ turns out to be the true initial resource stock. We shall only study this case with the simplifying assumption that $-q_1 = q_2 = q = \bar{S}-S^*$ and $\pi_1 = \pi_2 = 1/2$, i.e. the situation illustrated in figure 7.1. In figure 7.2 we have drawn the same curves m, l^* and l^{**} as in figure 7.1. In addition we have drawn a horizontal dotted curve representing c. From (7.4) and (7.5) it is clear that the right hand side of (7.4) multiplied by (1+r) is equal to the weighted average of $\text{Min}[c,\phi'(\bar{S}+q_i-\hat{x}_1) + (\bar{S}+q_i-\hat{x}_1)\phi''(\bar{S}+q_1-\hat{x}_1)]$ for all i. In the present case, assuming $\pi^*_1 = \pi_1 = 1/2$ at first, this means that the right hand side of (7.4) (multiplied by (1+r)) is represented by the line l', which is equally distanced from l^{**} and *either* c or l^*, whichever is lowest. Note that l' coincides with l from

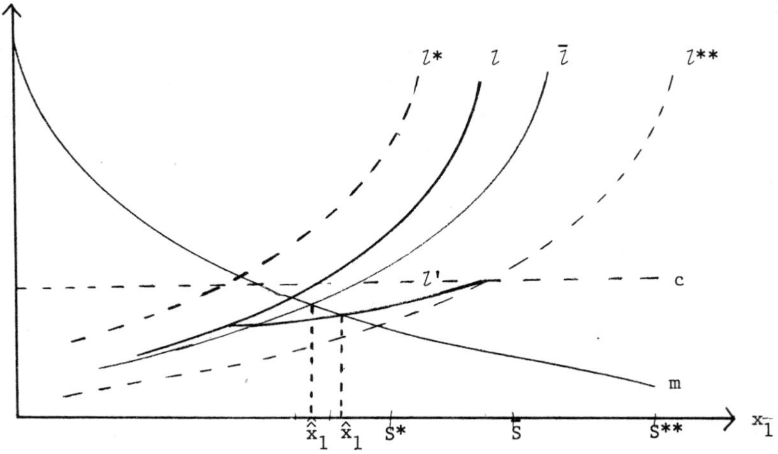

Figure 7.2

figure 7.1 for all values of x_1 which are so low that l^{**} and l^* lie below c. For higher values of x_1, l' will lie below l, and may well lie below $\bar{l}$ for sufficiently high values of x_1. From this reasoning it is clear that we may well get $\hat{x}_1 > \hat{\hat{x}}_1$, **like in figure 7.2, even if the** marginal revenue function is strictly convex. If the marginal revenue function is concave, we must always get $\hat{x}_1 > \hat{\hat{x}}_1$, because l' lies lower than l and l lies lower than $\bar{l}$ (or equal to $\bar{l}$ if the marginal revenue function is linear) in this case.

Let us now see how a slight increase in the degree of uncertainty, i.e. increased q, will affect $\hat{x}_1$. Since l^* lies above c for values of x_1 close to $\hat{x}_1$, a shift to the left of l^* (because of S* decreasing) will not affect l'. However the shift to the right of l^{**} (because S** increases) will make l' shift downwords. But this means that increasing the degree of uncertainty will increase the resource extraction in period 1, no matter how the curvature of the monopolist's marginal revenue function is.

It may seem strange that a small increase in the degree of uncertainty always will increase $\hat{x}_1$, while going from the case of certinty to the case with uncertainty could give a lower $\hat{x}_1$. However, the reasoning with a small increase in the degree of uncertainty assumed that the initial situation was such that whether or not the substitute would be produced in period 2 depended on what S turned out to be. Such an initial situation is of course logically impossible if S is known with certainty, the reasoning with a small increase in q used above is therefore not valid when q = 0 initially.

Finally, let us look at how risk aversion affects the monopolist's resource extraction. Like before, increasing the probability of the least desirable outcome is equivilant to shifting l' upwards, i.e. giving the possible outcome S = S** less weight. The effect of shifting l' upwards is of course a decrease in $\hat{x}_1$. Like before we can therefore conclude that the monopolist's optimal extraction in period 1 is lower if he has risk aversion than if he is risk neutral.

We saw that when (7.7) was valid, so that $\hat{x}_1$ followed from (7.6) with equality, the monopolist's initial resource extraction was lower than what was socially optimal. The same conclusion does not hold for all demand functions when (7.7) is not valid; in such cases it is possible to construct examples which imply that the monopolist extracts more than what is socially optimal in period 1. Like before, however, it is easy to find a sufficient condition for the monopolistic extraction in period 1 to be lower than what is socially optimal. To find such a condition, denote the optimal and monopolistic extraction by $\hat{x}_1^o$ and $\hat{x}_1^m$, respectively. From $r \geqq 0$, (6.3) and (6.8) we have $\hat{x}_1^o \geqq S^{**} - S^*/2 > S^{**}/2 > S^*/2$, which implies $\phi'(S^{**} - \hat{x}_1^o) \geqq \phi'(S^{**} - S^*/2) > c$. Together with (6.8) this gives us

$$(7.11) \qquad (1+r)\phi'(\hat{x}_1^o) < \phi'(S^{**}-\hat{x}_1^o).$$

When (7.7) is not valid (otherwise we know that $\hat{x}_1^m < \hat{x}_1^o$), it follows from (7.4) and (7.5) that

$$(1+r)[\phi'(\hat{x}_1^m) + \hat{x}_1^m\phi''(\hat{x}_1^m)] > \phi'(S^{**}-\hat{x}_1^m) + (S^{**}-\hat{x}_1^m)\phi''(S^{**}-\hat{x}_1^m).$$

Using (4.8) this can be rewritten as

$$[1 - \frac{1}{\eta(\hat{x}_1^m)}](1+r)\phi'(\hat{x}_1^m) > [1 - \frac{1}{\eta(S^{**}-\hat{x}_1^m)}]\phi'(S^{**}-\hat{x}_1^m).$$

If $\hat{x}_1^m < S^{**}-\hat{x}_1^m$, we must have $\hat{x}_1^m < \hat{x}_1^o$ (since $\hat{x}_1^o > S^{**}/2$, see above). If $\hat{x}_1^m \geqq S^{**} - \hat{x}_1^m$, the inequality above together with the assumption $\eta'(x) \leqq 0$ gives us

$$(7.12) \qquad (1+r)\phi'(\hat{x}_1^m) > \phi'(S^{**}-\hat{x}_1^m).$$

Comparing (7.12) with (7.11), it is clear that we must have $\hat{x}_1^m < \hat{x}_1^o$. In other words, a sufficient condition for the monopoly case to have a lower initial extraction is that the demand elasticity is a non-decreasing function of the price. In particular, it is clear that this condition is satisfied for linear and log-linear demand functions.

7.2. Linear demand function.

With our linear demand function (2.7) we have

$$\phi'(x) + x\phi''(x) = a - 2bx, \tag{7.13}$$

which together with (7.6) gives us

$$\hat{x}_1 \geqq \frac{a-(1+r)^{-1}c}{2b} \tag{7.14}$$

as long as this does not violate our condition $\hat{x}_1 \leqq S^*$.

The condition (7.7) may now be written

$$a - 2b(S^{**}-\hat{x}_1) \geqq c,$$

or

$$\hat{x}_1 \geqq S^{**}- \frac{a-c}{2b} \ . \tag{7.15}$$

If this condition holds, the substitute will be produced in period 2 no matter what S turns out to be. In this case $\hat{x}_1$ is given by (7.14) with an equality sign.

The condition (7.10) may now be written

$$(7.16) \qquad \hat{x}_1 \leqq S^* - \frac{a-c}{2b}.$$

If this condition holds, the substitute will not be produced in period 2 no matter what S turns out to b. In this case $\hat{x}_1$ is given by (7.9), which naw may be written

$$a - 2b\hat{x}_1 = (1+r)^{-1}\Sigma_i\pi_i^*[a-2b(\bar{S}+q_i-\hat{x}_1)],$$

or

$$(7.17) \qquad \hat{x}_1 = \frac{ar+2b\bar{S}+2b\Sigma_i\pi_i^*q_i}{(2+r)2b} .$$

We know that

$$\Sigma_i\pi_i^*q_i \leqq \Sigma_i\pi_iq_i = 0,$$

(7.17) therefore implies that

$$(7.18) \qquad \hat{x}_1 \leqq \frac{ar+2b\bar{S}}{(2+r)2b} ,$$

where the equation sign holds if and only if the monopolist is risk neutral. In other words, the only property of the distribution of S which affects $\hat{x}_1$ when the monopolist is risk neutral, is the expected value of S. (This statement is of course only true as long as (7.16) is valid.)

Let us finally consider the case where neither (7.15) nor (7.16) is valid. Like before, we shall only consider the case where $S = S^*$ with probability π and $S = S^{**}$ with probability $1 - \pi$. If and only if S^* turns out to be the true value of S in this case, substitute production will take place in period 2. From (7.4), (7.5) and (7.13) we see that the solution in this case is given by

$$(1+r)(a-2b\hat{x}_1) = \pi^*c + (1-\pi^*)(a-2bS^{**}+2b\hat{x}_1),$$

or

$$(7.19) \qquad \hat{x}_1 = \frac{ra+\pi^*(a-c)+(1-\pi^*)2bS^{**}}{(2+r-\pi^*)2b} .$$

Comparing (7.19) with (4.16), we see that these equations are identical except that the certain S in (4.16) has been substituted by the highest possible resource stock in (7.19). The reason for the similarity is the following: While the resource stock was considered certain in section 4, the probability of substitute produkction becoming technically feasible, and therefore also economically profitable due to the assumptions giving (4.16), was π. In the present case substitute production is known to be technically feasible, but it will only be economically profitable if the resource stock turns out to be S^*, which will occur with probability π. In other words, in both cases substitute production will occur in period 2 with the probability π, and if substitute production does <u>not</u> occur, the marginal revenue will be determined by S and S^{**}, respectively, in the two cases.

Turning to our numerical example with parameters as in chapter 6 (cf. pp. 77-78), direct calculation shows us that the inequality (7.14) violates $\hat{x}_1 \leqq S^*$ when $S^* = 40$. This means that $\hat{x}_1 = S^* = 40$ irrespectively of whether or not the monopolist has risk aversion, both for $r = 0,5$ and $r = 0$. If $S^* = \bar{S} = S^{**} = 55$, the inequality (7.14) would not be contradicted by $\hat{x}_1 \leq S^*$. Furthermore, it is easily verified that in this case the solution for $\hat{x}_1$ follows from (7.14) with an equation sign, as this solution does not violate (7.15). Our solutions in the case of uncertainty as well as certainty are summarized in table 7.1.

Resource extraction ($\hat{x}_1$) with full monopoly (linear demand function given by (2.7) and (2.12)).

q \ r	0,5	0
30	40	40
0	48,9	45,2

Table 7.1

Just like in the competitive and optimal solution, the present solution implies that as much as possible is extracted in the first period when the true total initial resource stock is uncertain.

7.3. Log-linear demand function.

With our log-linear demand function (2.13) we have

$$(7.20) \qquad \phi'(x) + x\phi''(x) = (1-\beta)Ax^{-\beta},$$

which together with (7.6) gives us

$$(7.21) \qquad \hat{x}_1 \geqq \left[\frac{c}{(1+r)(1-\beta)A}\right]^{-1/\beta},$$

as long as this does not violate our condition $\hat{x}_1 \leqq S^*$.

The condition (7.7) may now be written

$$(1-\beta)A(S^{**}-\hat{x}_1)^{-\beta} \geqq c$$

or

$$\hat{x}_1 \geqq S^{**} - [\frac{c}{(1-\beta)A}]^{-1/\beta} . \qquad (7.22)$$

If this condition holds, the substitute will be produced in period 2 no matter what S turns out to be. In this case $\hat{x}_1$ is given by (7.21) with an equality sign.

The condition (7.8) may now be written

$$\hat{x}_1 \leqq S^{*} - [\frac{c}{(1-\beta)A}]^{-1/\beta} . \qquad (7.23)$$

If this condition holds, the substitute will not be produced in period 2 no matter what S turns out to be. In this case $\hat{x}_1$ is given by (7.9), which may be written

$$(1-\beta)A\hat{x}_1^{-\beta} = (1+r)^{-1}\Sigma_i\pi_i^*[(1-\beta)A(\bar{S}+q_i-\hat{x}_1)^{-\beta}],$$

or

$$(1+r)\hat{x}_1^{-\beta} = \Sigma_i\pi_i^*(\bar{S}+q_i-\hat{x}_1)^{-\beta}. \qquad (7.24)$$

Since (7.20) is strictly convex and

$$\Sigma_i\pi_i^*q_i \leqq \Sigma_i\pi_iq_i = 0,$$

(7.24) implies that

$$(7.25) \qquad (1+r)\hat{x}_1^{-\beta} \geqq (\bar{S} - \hat{x}_1)^{-\beta} ,$$

where the equality sign is valid if and only if there is no uncertainty, i.e. $S^* = S^{**} = \bar{S}$. Unlike the case with a linear demand function, $\hat{x}_1$ will depend not only on $\bar{S}$, but also on all q_i and π_i, even when the monopolist is risk neutral.

Let us finally consider the case where neither (7.22) nor (7.23) is valid. Like before, we shall only consider the case where $S = S^*$ with probability π and $S = S^{**}$ with probability $1 - \pi$. If and only if S^* turns out to be the true value of S in this case, substitute production will take place in period 2. From (7.4), (7.5) and (7.20) we see that the solution in this case is given by

$$(1+r)(1-\beta)A\hat{x}_1^{-\beta} = \pi^*c + (1-\pi\ )(1-\beta)A(S^{**}-\hat{x}_1)^{-\beta}$$

or

$$(7.26) \qquad (1+r)\hat{x}_1^{-\beta} = \pi^*\frac{c}{(1-\beta)A} + (1-\pi^*)(S^{**}-\hat{x}_1)^{-\beta}.$$

Comparing this equation with (4.20), we see that they are practically identical, the only difference being that S in (4.20) is substituted by S^{**} in (7.26). The reason for this similarity is of course the same as the reason for the similarity between (4.16) and (7.19), discussed in section 7.2 (p. 90).

Using our numerical values for A, β, c and r, it is easy to see that (7.21) is not violated by $\hat{x}_1 \leqq S^*$ when $S^* = 40$ or when $S^* = \bar{S} = 55$. However, neither in the case of uncertainty nor in the case of certainty will $\hat{x}_1$ be given by (7.21) with an equality sign, as this solution would violate (7.22). It turns out that our solutions in all cases (r = 0,5 and r = 0, certain and uncertain resource stock, risk neutrality and risk aversion) and given by (7.24), as these values of $\hat{x}_1$ satisfy the inequality (7.23). The results are given in table 7.2.

Resource extraction ($\hat{x}_1$) with full monopoly (log-linear demand function given by (2.14) and (2.17).

q, π^* \ r		0,5	0
q=30	$\pi^* = 1/2$	28,6	24,0
	$\pi^* = 3/4$	26,2	21,7
	$\pi^* = 1$	24,4	20,0
q = 0		33,7	27,5

Table 7.2

From table 7.2 we see that the initial resource extraction is lower in the case of uncertainty than in the case of certainty. Risk aversion means increasing the weight of the least desirable outcome, which implies that $\pi^* > \pi = 1/2$ in the case of risk aversion (remembering that π^* in our formulas is the adjusted probability of the lowest possible S-value occuring). From table 7.1 we see that the numerical importance of introducing risk aversion is not large.

7.4. Summary of chapter 7.

Our assumptions implied that it always would be socially optimal to produce the substitute in period 2. However, a monopolist controlling the substitute as well as the resource might find it profitable - for some or all results of the exploration activity - not to produce the substitute in period 2. *If* the distribution of the uncertain size of the resource stock is such that the monopolist will produce the substitute no matter what the true size of the stock turns out to be, we can draw the following conclusion: Just like in the competitive and socially optimal solution, the monopolist's extraction in period 1 will be independent of all properties of the probability distribution of the size of the resource stock, unless the monopolist's extraction is equal to the total stock available for extraction in the first period. Furthermore, the extraction in this case will be unaffected by whether or not the monopolist has risk aversion.

Let us now turn to the case where the monopolist will find it profitable not to produce the substitute in period 2 for some or all outcomes of what the true size of the resource stock is. In this case the initial resource extraction may be lower or higher than it would have been if the resource stock was known with certainty to be equal to its expected value. A necessary, but not sufficient, condition for the initial resource extraction to be lower in the case of uncertainty and risk neutrality than in the case of certainty is that the marginal revenue function is strictly convex, at least in some region between the two solutions. In the numerical examples studied in section 7.3 we found that whenever the monopoly solution in the case of uncertainty was not a corner solution, this solution had a lower extraction in period 1 than the corresponding solution with a certain resource stock.

Whenever risk aversion affects the monopolist's solution, the initial resource extraction will be lower in the case of risk aversion than in the case of risk neutrality. From what we have said above it therefore follows that if the initial extraction depends on the monopolist's degree of risk aversion and the marginal revenue function is strictly concave, the strength of risk aversion will be decisive for whether the initial extraction in the case of uncertainty will be higher or lower than in the case of certainty.

One cannot conclude that the present monopoly case always will have a lower initial resource extraction than the competitive and optimal solution. However, this will be the case for most reasonable specifications of the demand function, especially when the monopoly has risk aversion. In particular, this conclusion holds both for linear and log-linear demand functions.

CHAPTER 8.
MONOPOLY OF THE RESOURCE WITH AN UNCERTAIN RESOURCE STOCK.

8.1. The general case.

Like before, the monopolist maximizes

$$(8.1) \qquad EV^*(x_1,S) = x_1\phi'(x_1) + (1+r)^{-1}EV_2^*(x_1,S),$$

where $V_2(x_1,S)$ is the maximal profit in period 2 given that x_1 is extracted in period 1 and that the true initial resource stock turns out to be S. More precisely, in the present case we have

$$(8.2) \qquad V_2(x_1,S) = (S-x_1)\text{Min}[c,\ \phi'(S-x_1)]$$ [1)]

and

$$(8.3) \qquad EV_2^*(x_1,S) = \Sigma_i\ \pi_i^*V_2(x_1,\ \bar{S}+q_i).$$

Just like in the case of full monopoly, all π_i^*'s depend on the optimal x_1. Also in the present case the sign of $(\pi_i^* - \pi_i)q_i$ depends on which outcomes of S are considered as most desirable by the monopolist. Since the monopolist can choose how much of the remaining resource stock to extract in period 2, a higher S is never regarded as less desirable than a lower S. Furthermore, except for outcomes of S which are so high that it is not profitable to

---

1) This equation only holds for $\partial V_2(x_1,S)/\partial S \geq 0$, i.e. as long as a marginal increase in the resource stock increases profits. If this inequality does not hold for some values of $S-x_1$, we get $V_2(x_1,S) = \hat{Z}\phi'(\hat{Z}) = \underset{Z\geqq 0}{\text{Max}}[Z\phi'(Z)]$ for these values. For outcomes of S that are so high that $\partial V_2(\hat{x}_1,S)/\partial S < 0$, an amount $S-\hat{x}_1-\hat{Z}$ of the resource stock will remain unextracted after period 2.

extract all the remaining stock in period 2 (cf. footnote 1, p. 233), the monopolist will consider the outcomes with higher S as more desirable than outcomes with lower S. Like before, we therefore must have $(\pi_i^* - \pi_i)q_i \leqq 0$, where a strict inequality holds when $q_i \neq 0$ and sufficiently low to make it profitable to extract $\bar{S}+q_i-\hat{x}_1$ and the monopolist is risk averse.

Before proceeding, let us prove that there exist outcomes of S which have the following two properties: (a) All of the remaining resource stock from period 1 is extracted in period 2, and (b) the resource price in period 2 is equal to c. To prove that such outcomes of S are possible, consider the outcome S*. Assume that (a) above does not hold, i.e. that the resource extraction in period 2 $(=\hat{x}_2)$ is smaller than $S^* - \hat{x}_1$. If this is true for S*, which is the smallest possible outcome of S, it must be optimal to have the extraction in period 2 smaller than $S - \hat{x}_1$ for all outcomes of S (due to concavity). This means that the resource constraint is non-binding, giving the following equations for $\hat{x}_1$ and $\hat{x}_2$:

$$\phi'(\hat{x}_1) + \hat{x}_1\phi'(\hat{x}_1) = 0$$

(8.4)

$$\phi'(\hat{x}_2) + \hat{x}_2\phi'(\hat{x}_2) \leqq 0.$$

But from (6.2) (with $c_1=0$) and the fact that $x\phi'(x)$ is concave it is clear that (8.4) implies $\hat{x}_i > S^{**} - S^*/2 > S^*/2$, i=1,2. So our assumption that $\hat{x}_1 + \hat{x}_2 < S^*$ implies that $\hat{x}_1 + \hat{x}_2 > S^*$. This contradiction proves (a) above. As for (b), we must have $\phi'(S^* - \hat{x}_1) < c$ if (b) is not true for the outcome S*. But if this is true for S*, $\phi'(S-\hat{x}_1) < c$ must be true for all outcomes of S. In other words, the existence of a substitute is not an effective constraint for the monopolist. But then we must have $\hat{x}_1 > S^*/2$, i.e. $S^* - \hat{x}_1 < S^* - S^*/2 < S^{**} - S^*/2$, giving $\phi'(S^* - \hat{x}_1) > \phi'(S^{**} - S^*/2) > c$ due to (6.3). This contradiction proves that (b) must be true.

The function $EV^*(x_1,S)$ is a strictly concave, continuous function of x_1. However, it is not differentiable in x_1 at the points where $\phi'(\bar{S}+q_i-x_1) = c$. Distinguishing between left and right hand derivatives, the solution $\hat{x}_1$ must imply

$$\frac{\partial EV^*(\hat{x}_1,S)}{\partial x_1^-} \geqq 0 \qquad \text{and} \qquad \frac{\partial EV^*(\hat{x}_1,S)}{\partial x_1^+} \leqq 0$$

Using (8.1) and (8.3) this means that

$$(8.5)\quad \begin{cases} \phi'(\hat{x}_1) + \hat{x}_1\phi''(\hat{x}_1) \geqq -(1+r)^{-1}\,\Sigma_i\,\pi_i^*\,\dfrac{\partial V_2^*(\hat{x}_1,\,\bar{S}+q_i)}{\partial x_1^-} \\[2ex] \phi'(\hat{x}_1) + \hat{x}_1\phi''(\hat{x}_1) \leqq -(1+r)^{-1}\,\Sigma_i\,\pi_i^*\,\dfrac{\partial V_2^*(\hat{x}_1,\,\bar{S}+q_i)}{\partial x_1^+}. \end{cases}$$

From (8.2) we know that $-\partial V_2^*(x_1,S)/\partial x_1^+ \leqq c$, it therefore follows from (8.5) that

$$(8.6)\qquad \phi'(\hat{x}_1) + \hat{x}_1\phi''(\hat{x}_1) \leqq (1+r)^{-1}c\ ,$$

which is identical to the inequality we had in the case of full monopoly (cf. (7.6)).

Let us look at the special case where $\phi'(\bar{S}+q_i-\hat{x}_1) > c$ whichever q_i turns out to be the true one. Since $S^{**} \geqq \bar{S}+q_i$ the inequality above will hold if and only if

$$(8.7)\qquad \phi'(S^{**} - \hat{x}_1) \ > \ c.$$

Since $\partial V_2^*(\hat{x}_1,\ S)/\partial x_1 = -c$ when $\phi'(S-\hat{x}_1) > c$, the monopolist's resource extraction follows from (8.6) with an equality sign if this solution implies that (8.7) is valid.

Notice that (7.7) implies, but is not implied by, (8.7). This means that whenever (7.7) holds for $\hat{x}_1$ determined by (7.6) (identical to (8.6)) with an equality sign, the solution to the two monopoly cases are identical, and both involve a lower initial resource extraction than what is socially optimal. If (8.7) holds, but (7.7) is *not* valid, the solution of the present case gives equality in (8.6), while the extraction of a monopoly controlling the backstop technology would make (8.6) valid with a strict inequality. This means that the initial extraction in the present case will be lower than the extraction in the case of full monopoly.

We now turn to the case where (8.7) is not valid. However, we shall restrict ourselves to the simple probability distribution where $-q_1 = q_2 = q = \bar{S} - S^*$ and $\pi_1 = \pi_2 = 1/2$, i.e. the same distribution as was assumed in figures 7.1 and 7.2. This case is easiest to treat graphically. In figure 8.1 we have illustrated the case of certainty, i.e. q=0. Like before, m represents $(1+r)[\phi'(x_1) + x_1\phi''(x_1)]$, and $\bar{l}$ stands for $\phi'(\bar{S}-x_1) + (\bar{S}-x_1)\phi''(\bar{S}-x_1)$. The line $\bar{h}$ represents $\phi'(\bar{S}-x_1)$, notice that $\bar{h}$ and c intersect to the left of the intersection between m and $\bar{l}$. This must always be the case, as $r \geqq 0$ implies that m and $\bar{l}$ intersect at some value of $x_1 \geqq \bar{S}/2$, while (6.3) implies that $\bar{h}$ and c intersect at some value $x_1 < \bar{S}/2$. We have assumed that $\bar{h}$ and c intersect to the right of the intersection between m and c. If this were not the case, our solution would follow from (8.6) with equality, which would satisfy (8.7). As this case already has been treated, we shall disregard it in the following analysis.

The discontinuous function $\partial V_2^*(\hat{x}_1,\bar{S})/\partial x_1$ which enters (8.5) is given by $\bar{l}$ to the left of the intersection between $\bar{h}$ and c, and is given by c to the right of this point. From (8.5) it is therefore clear that $\hat{x}_1$ must be given precisely by the value of x_1 making $\bar{h}$ and c intersect.

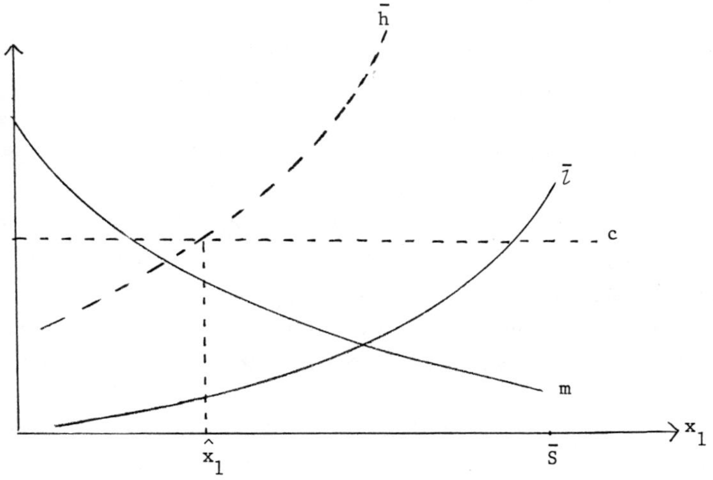

Figure 8.1

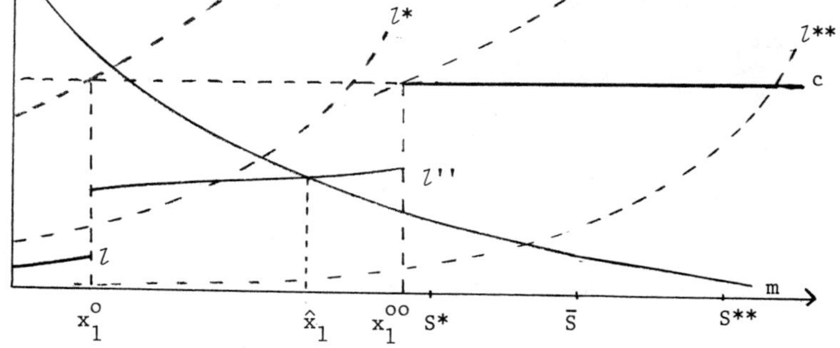

Figure 8.2

Let us now introduce uncertainty. Instead of $\bar{l}$ we then get the two curves l^* and l^{**}, where the horizontal difference between these curves is $S^{**} - S^* = 2(\bar{S} - S^*)$, see figure 8.2. Like before, l is equally distanced from l^* and l^{**}, measured vertically. The curve $\bar{h}$ is replaced by h^* and h^{**} in the same way as $\bar{l}$, l^* and l^{**}. The curves m and c are of course the same as they were in the case of certainty. In figure 8.2 we have drawn l^{**} above the x_1-axis for all $x_1 \geqq 0$. As indicated by the footnote on page 97, this need not be the case. If l^{**} lies below the x_1-axis for some x_1, our analysis is modified by using the x_1-axis instead of l^{**} for all x_1 where this is the case (cf. the footnote on page 97).

The discontinuous function $\partial EV_2^*(x_1,S)/\partial x_1$ which enters (8.5) is given by l to the left of x_1^o, which is the value of x_1 which makes h^* and c intersect. Between x_1^o and x_1^{oo}, $\partial EV_2^*(x_1,S)/\partial x_1$ is given by l'', which is equally distanced from c and l^{**}, measured vertically. Notice that l'' lies above l to the left of the intersection between l^* and c, and below l to the right of this intersection point. To the right of x_1^{oo}, which is the value of x_1 making h^{**} and c intersect, $\partial EV_2^*(x_1,S)/\partial x_1$ is given by c. The solution $\hat{x}_1$ is found in the intersection between m and the broken curve representing $\partial EV_2^*(x_1,S)/\partial x_1$.

From figure 8.2 it is clear that there are four possible types of solutions, depending on how m lies compared with l^*, l^{**}, h^*, h^{**} and c, which depends on q and r, among other things. These four types of solutions are (i) $\hat{x}_1 = x_1^o$, (ii) $\hat{x}_1 = x_1^{oo}$, (iii) $x_1^o < \hat{x}_1 < x_1^{oo}$ and (iv) $\hat{x}_1 > x_1^{oo}$. The last of these will occur if (8.7) holds, and has already been treated. Let us study the other three solutions somewhat closer.

From figure 8.2 we find that x_1^o and x_1^{oo} are given by

$$\phi'(S^* - x_1^o) = c \tag{8.8}$$

and

$$\phi'(S^{**} - x_1^{oo}) = c. \tag{8.9}$$

From (8.5) we see that x_1^o is our solution if

$$\phi'(x_1^o) + x_1^o\phi''(x_1^o) \leqq -(1+r)^{-1}[\pi^* \frac{\partial V_2^*(x_1^o,S^*)}{\partial x_1^+} + (1-\pi^*) \frac{\partial V_2^*(x_1^o,S^{**})}{\partial x_1^+}]$$ 1)

i.e.

(8.10) $$\phi'(x_1^o) + x_1^o\phi''(x_1^o) \leqq (1+r)^{-1}[\pi^*c + (1-\pi^*)(\phi'(S^{**}-x_1^o) + (S^{**}-x_1^o)\phi''(S^{**}-x_1^o))] .$$

Similarly, x_1^{oo} is our solution if $\hat{x}_1 = x_1^{oo}$ satisfies both inequalities in (8.5), i.e. if

(8.11) $$\phi'(x_1^{oo}) + x_1^{oo}\phi''(x_1^{oo}) \leqq (1+r)^{-1}c$$

and

(8.12) $$\phi'(x_1^{oo}) + x_1^{oo}\phi''(x_1^{oo}) \geqq (1+r)^{-1}[\pi^*c + (1-\pi^*)(\phi'(S^{**}-x_1^{oo}) + (S^{**}-x_1^{oo})\phi''(S^{**}-x_1^{oo}))].$$

If neither of the two inequalities (8.10) and (8.12) hold, the solution $\hat{x}_1$ is somewhere in the open interval (x_1^o, x_1^{oo}). More precisely, the solution in this case is given by

(8.13) $$\phi'(\hat{x}_1) + \hat{x}_1\phi''(\hat{x}_1) = (1+r)^{-1}[\pi^*c + (1-\pi^*)(\phi'(S^{**}-\hat{x}_1) + (S^{**}-\hat{x}_1)\phi''(S^{**}-\hat{x}_1))].$$

---

1) The other inequality in (8.5) will always be satisfied due to our proof that we must have $\phi'(S^*-\hat{x}_1) \geqq c$, cf. p. 98, which excludes the possibility of $\hat{x}_1 < x_1^o$.

Finally, if (8.12) holds (which implies that (8.10) does not hold), but (8.11) does not hold, we have $\hat{x}_1 > x_1^{oo}$. More precisely, in this case $\hat{x}_1$ is given by (8.6) with equality, which is a case we already have treated.

Let us compare the solution of the present monopoly case with the solution in the case of full monopoly when π^* is the same in both cases. The resource extraction in the case of full monopoly was given by the intersection of the curve m and the lowest of the curves c and l', where l' never was above l (see figure 7.2). Our present solution is given by the intersection between m and the broken curve $l - l'' - c$, cf. figure (8.2). The lines l' and l'' are identical to the right of the intersection point between l^* and c. For values of x_1 between the intersection of l^* and c and h** and c (if any), as well as for values of x_1 higher than the intersection between l^{**} and c, the relevant curve l'-c in the case of full monopoly and $l - l'' - c$ in the present case are identical. For all other values of $x_1 > x_1^o$ the broken curve l''-c lies above the curve l'-c, see figure (8.2)[1]. We can therefore conclude that the initial resource extraction will be lower or equal in the present case than in the case of full monopoly.

As usual, we cannot give an unambigious answer to the question of whether or not the present monopoly solution will imply less initial extraction than what is socially optimal. However, from the comparison above with the case of full monopoly and a result in section 7.1 (pp. 86-88), we can draw the following conclusion: A sufficient condition for the present monopoly case to have a lower initial extraction than what is socially optimal is that the demand elasticity is a non-decreasing function of the price.

Before comparing the case of uncertainty with the case of certainty, it is convenient to study the effect of a small increase in the degree of uncertainty, i.e. a small increase in q. This will move S*, h* and l^* to the left and S**, h** and l^{**} to the right (see figure 8.2). From figure 8.2 we see that this implies that x_1^o moves to the left and x_1^{oo} moves to the right. Furthermore, since l''devides c and l^{**} in the proportion $\pi^*/(1-\pi^*)$, l'' moves downwards when l^{**} moves to the right. We can therefore conclude from figure 1 that if $x_1^o < \hat{x}_1 \leqq x_1^{oo}$ initially, a small increase

1) Notice that x_1^o cannot be a solution in the case of full monopoly. This follows from (8.8) and (6.3), which imply $x_1^o < S^*/2$, which cannot be a solution satisfying (7.4) and (7.5) when $r \geqq 0$.

in the degree of uncertainty will increase the resource extraction in period 1. If $\hat{x}_1 = x_1^o$ initially, a small increase in q will decrease $\hat{x}_1$ if m initially lies below l'' at x_1^o, and increase $\hat{x}_1$, if m initially touches l'' at x_1^o.[1)]

Let us now start with q=0 and give q a small increase. When q=0, l^*, l^{**}, l and $\bar{l}$ are identical, and $\hat{x}_1 \geqq x_1^o = x_1^{oo}$. If $\hat{x}_1 > x_1^o = x_1^{oo}$, an increased q will leave $\hat{x}_1$ unchanged (determined by the intersection of m and c) for a sufficiently small change in q. An increase in q will move x_1^{oo} to the right, and for a sufficiently large increase in q, x_1^{oo} will move to the right of the initial $\hat{x}_1$, so that $\hat{x}_1$ will increase to the new value of x_1^{oo} or to the intersection between m and l''.

Assume now that $\hat{x}_1 = x_1^o = x_1^{oo}$ when q=0. A small increase in q will mean that x_1^o moves to the left and x_1^{oo} to the right, leaving a short line l'', lying above the original $\bar{l}$, between x_1^o and x_1^{oo}. A careful inspection of the figures 8.1 and 8.2 reveals that a small increase in q will make $\hat{x}_1$ follow x_1^{oo}, i.e. increase, or follow x_1^o, i.e. decrease, depending on whether m is closest to c or $\bar{l}$ at the initial $\hat{x}_1$ (assuming $\pi^* = \pi = 1/2$). If m lies exactly in the middle of c and $\bar{l}$ at the initial $\hat{x}_1$, an increase in q, no matter how small, will give a solution for $\hat{x}_1$ determined by the intersection between m and l'', which means that $\hat{x}_1$ increases.

From the discussion above it is clear that comparing a situation with uncertainty with the case of a certain resource stock, there is no unambiguous answer to the question about which case implies the highest initial resource extraction. Furthermore, unlike the case of full monopoly, the answer to the question above will never depend on whether the marginal revenue function is convex of concave. The same applies to the question about the effect of increasing the degree of uncertainty; no unambiguous answer exists, and the answer does not depend on whether or not the demand function is convex or concave. However, there is a tendency for increased uncertainty to increase the initial resource extraction: From the reasoning with figure 8.2 it is clear that this will be the case whenever $\hat{x}_1$ initially is higher than its lowest possible value (= x_1^o).

---

1) There is one exception to these results. We mentioned earlier (p. 97) that l^{**} could lie below the x_1-axis for some x_1 larger than x_1^o. For such values of x_1, l'' will simply be a horizontal line π^*c above the x_1-axis. This portion of l'' will of course not be affected by l^{**} shifting downwards, so that a solution $\hat{x}_1$ initially determined by the intersection of m and such a portion of l'' will stay unchanged when the degree of uncertainty is increased.

The effect of risk aversion on the resource extraction follows easily from figure 8.2. From what we have said earlier in this section (pp. 97-98), risk aversion means that $\pi^* > \pi = 1/2$ (where π is the probability of $S=S^*$). In figure 8.2 going from risk neutrality to risk aversion therefore means shifting l upwards (towards l^*) and l'' upwards (towards c). The points x_1^o and x_1^{oo} will not be affected by the introduction of risk aversion. It is therefore clear that if $\hat{x}_1 = x_1^o$ or $\hat{x}_1 > x_1^{oo}$ without risk aversion, introducing risk aversion will not affect $\hat{x}_1$. If $x_1^o < \hat{x}_1 < x_1^{oo}$ without risk aversion, introducing risk aversion will reduce $\hat{x}_1$. Finally, if $\hat{x}_1 = x_1^{oo}$ with risk neutrality, the introduction of risk aversion will leave $\hat{x}_1$ unchanged or reduce $\hat{x}_1$[1].

---

1) If m intersects c at x_1^{oo}, $\hat{x}_1$ will always be unaffected by the introduction of risk aversion. If m touches l'' at x_1^{oo}, introduction of risk aversion will always reduce $\hat{x}_1$. If m lies somewhere between c and l'' at x_1^{oo}, introducing risk aversion will leave $\hat{x}_1$ unchanged for a sufficiently weak degree of risk aversion, and reduce $\hat{x}_1$ for a sufficiently large degree of risk aversion.

8.2. Linear demand function.

With our linear demand function (2.7) we have

$$(8.14) \qquad \phi'(x) + x\phi''(x) = a - 2bx ,$$

which together with (8.6) gives us

$$(8.15) \qquad \hat{x}_1 \geqq \frac{a - (1+r)^{-1}c}{2b} ,$$

as long as this does not violate our condition $\hat{x}_1 \leqq S^*$.

The condition (8.7) may now be written

$$a - b(S^{**} - \hat{x}_1) > c,$$

or

$$(8.16) \qquad \hat{x}_1 > S^{**} - \frac{a-c}{b} .$$

If this condition holds, the substitute will be produced in period 2 no matter what S turns out to be. In this case $\hat{x}_1$ will be given by (8.15) with an equality sign.

If (8.16) does not hold, we must have $x_1^o \leqq \hat{x}_1 \leqq x_1^{oo}$. From (8.8) and (8.9) and our linear demand function it is clear that

$$(8.17) \qquad x_1^o = S^* - \frac{a-c}{b}$$

and

$$(8.18) \qquad x_1^{oo} = S^{**} - \frac{a-c}{b} .$$

The condition (8.10), which must be satisfied for x_1^o to be the solution, may be written, after some manupulation,

$$(8.19) \qquad x_1^o \geqq \frac{ra + \pi^*(a-c) + (1-\pi^*)2bS^{**}}{(2+r-\pi^*)2b} .$$

Together with (8.17) this gives a condition on S^* and S^{**}, or on $\bar{S}$ and q, remembering that $S^* = \bar{S}-q$ and $S^{**} = \bar{S}+q$. However, further manupulation of (8.17) and (8.19) does not give any easily interpretable results, and is therefore omitted.

The conditions (8.11) and (8.12), which must be satisfied for x_1^{oo} to be the solution, may be written as

$$(8.20) \qquad \frac{ra + (a-c)}{(1+r)2b} \leqq x_1^{oo} \leqq \frac{ra + \pi^*(a-c) + (1-\pi^*)2bS^{**}}{(2+r-\pi^*)2b} .$$

If neither of the conditions (8.16), (8.19) and (8.20) hold, the solution is given by (8.13), which in the present case may be written as

$$(8.21) \qquad \hat{x}_1 = \frac{ra + \pi^*(a-c) + (1-\pi^*)2bS^{**}}{(2+r-\pi^*)2b} .$$

This is the same solution as (7.19), which was a possible solution in the case of full monopoly. However, the conditions for when this solution is valid differs in the two cases. In the case of full monopoly it was valid if neither (7.15) nor (7.16) were valid, i.e. if

$$(8.22) \qquad S^* \leqq \hat{x}_1 + \frac{a-c}{2b} \leqq S^{**} ,$$

while (8.21) is valid in the present case if and only if it satisfies $x_1^o \leqq \hat{x}_1 \leqq x_1^{oo}$, i.e. if and only if

$$(8.23) \qquad S^* \leqq \hat{x}_1 + \frac{a-c}{b} \leqq S^{**}.$$

Notice that the interval of possible $\hat{x}_1$-values satisfying (8.23) lies to the left of the corresponding interval satisfying (8.22). The interval given by (8.23) is illustrated by the interval between x_1^o and x_1^{oo} in figure 8.2, while the interval in (8.22) is illustrated be the interval between the intersection of l^* and c and of l^{**} and c. Wheather or not these intervals will overlap will depend on the degree of uncertainty.

Turning to our numerical example with parameters given in chapter 6 (cf. pp. 77-78) direct calculation shows us that the inequality (8.15) violates $\hat{x}_1 \leqq S^*$ when $S^*=40$. This means that $\hat{x}_1 = S^* = 40$ irrespectively of whether or not the monopolist has risk aversion, both for r=0,5 and r=0. If $S^* = \bar{S} = S^{**} = 55$, the inequality (8.15) would not be contradicted by $\hat{x}_1 \leqq S^*$. Furthermore, it is easily verified that in this case the solution for $\hat{x}_1$ follows from (8.15) with an equation sign, as this solution does not violate (8.16). Our solutions in the present monopoly case therefore turn out to be identical to the solutions in the case of full monopoly, summarized in table 7.1.

8.3. Log-linear demand function.

With our log-linear demand function (2.13) we have

$$(8.24) \qquad \phi'(x) + x\phi''(x) \;=\; (1-\beta)Ax^{-\beta} ,$$

which together with (8.6) gives us

$$(8.25) \qquad \hat{x}_1 \;\geqq\; \left[\frac{c}{(1+r)(1-\beta)A}\right]^{-\frac{1}{\beta}} ,$$

as long as this does not violate our condition $\hat{x}_1 \leqq S^*$.

The condition (8.7) may now be written

$$A(S^{**} - \hat{x}_1)^{-\beta} \;>\; c$$

or

$$(8.26) \qquad \hat{x}_1 \;>\; S^{**} - \left(\frac{c}{A}\right)^{-\frac{1}{\beta}} .$$

If this condition holds, the substitute will be produced in period 2 no matter what S turns out to be. In this case $\hat{x}_1$ will be given by (8.25) with an equality sign.

If (8.26) does not hold, we must have $x_1^{o} \leqq \hat{x}_1 \leqq x_1^{oo}$. From (8.8) and (8.9) and our log-linear demand function it is clear that

$$(8.27) \qquad x_1^{o} \;=\; S^* - \left(\frac{c}{A}\right)^{-\frac{1}{\beta}}$$

and

$$(8.28)\qquad x_1^{oo} = S^{**} - \left(\frac{c}{A}\right)^{-\frac{1}{\beta}} .$$

The condition (8.10), which must be satisfied for x_1^o to be the solution, may be written in the following way in the present case:

$$(8.29)\qquad (1+r)(x_1^o)^{-\beta} \leqq \pi^* \frac{c}{(1-\beta)A} + (1-\pi^*)(S^{**} - x_1^o)^{-\beta} .$$

Similarly, the conditions (8.11) and (8.12), which must be satisfied for x_1^{oo} to be the solution, now become

$$(8.30)\qquad x_1^{oo} \geqq \left[\frac{c}{(1+r)(1-\beta)A}\right]^{-\frac{1}{\beta}}$$

and

$$(8.31)\qquad (1+r)(x_1^{oo})^{-\beta} \geqq \pi^* \frac{c}{(1-\beta)A} + (1-\pi^*)(S^{**} - x_1^{oo})^{-\beta}.$$

If the solution neither is x_1^o, x_1^{oo} or given by (8.25) with equality, the solution follows from

$$(8.32)\qquad (1+r)(\hat{x}_1)^{-\beta} = \pi^* \frac{c}{(1-\beta)A} + (1-\pi^*)(S^{**} - \hat{x}_1)^{-\beta} .$$

Like in the case with a linear demand function, this solution is identical to a possible solution in the case of full monopoly (see (7.26)). However, the conditions which must hold for (8.32) to be a solution are different for the two monopoly cases. The different conditions could be compared in more detail, like we did in the case of a linear demand function. However, little new insight is gained by repeating this procedure, and it is therefore omitted.

Using our numerical values for A, β, c and r, it is easy to see that (8.25) is not violated by $\hat{x}_1 \leqq S^*$ when $S^*=40$ or when $S^* = \bar{S} = 55$. Furthermore, in the case of certainty (i.e. $S^* = \bar{S} = S^{**} = 55$) it turns out that $\hat{x}_1$ follows from (8.25) with an equality sign, as this does not violate (8.26). In the case of uncertainty, however, (8.25) with equality will violate (8.26) both for r=0,5 and r=0. It turns out that both for r=0,5 and r=0, and whatever value in the interval [1/2,1] π^* has, the solution is in the open interval (x_1^o, x_1^{oo}), i.e. given by (8.32). The results are summarized in table 8.1

Resource extraction ($\hat{x}_1$) with a resource extracting monopolist (log-linear demand function given by (2.14) and (2.17)).

q, π^* \ r		0,5	0
q=30	π^* = 1/2	12,4	8,0
	π^* = 3/4	8,5	5,4
	π^* = 1	6,4	4,1
q=0		6,4	4,1

Table 8.1

Comparing table 8.1 with table 7,1, it is clear that the two monopoly cases are very different. First, we notice that with or without uncertainty, with or without risk aversion, and whichever discount rate is used, the monopolist not controlling the substitute has a much lower resource extraction in the first period than a monopolist also controlling substitute production. Furthermore, in the case of full monopoly we found that uncertainty had the effect of decreasing the initial resource extraction. From table 8.1 we see that the opposite is true for the case where the substitute is supplied competitively. In both cases we find that risk aversion has the effect of reducing the initial resource extraction, compared with the case of risk neutrality. In particular, we see from table

8.1 that for the limiting case of infinitly high risk aversion ($\pi^*=1$), the monopolist extracts the same amount in period 1 when the size of the resource stock is uncertain as when this size is known with certainty.

8.4. Summary of chapter 8.

Comparing the present monopoly case with the case of full monopoly, we find that the initial resource extraction (for the same π^*) never can exceed the initial extraction in the case of full monopoly. The resource extraction may be identical in the two cases, like we found for the numerical examples with a linear demand function, or the present case may have less extraction in the first period than the extraction with full monopoly, like we found for the numerical examples with a log-linear demand function.

In chapter 7 we showed that the case of full monopoly would usually have a lower initial resource extraction than what was socially optimal. Together with the conclusion above this means that one will expect to find a monopolist not controlling the substitute extracting less in the first period than what is optimal. However, there exist cases where the opposite is true, i.e. where the monopolist extracts more than what is socially optimal in the first period. In our examples with a linear demand function the monopolist's extraction in the case of uncertainty was a high as physically possible in the first period, which also was the socially optimal solution. In our examples with a log-linear demand function the monopolist's initial resource extraction was much lower than the optimal extraction.

In the case of full monopoly we found that uncertainty could give a lower or higher initial extraction than the case of certainty. This result is valid also for the present monopoly case. However, in the present case the curvature of the marginal revenue function is not decisive for the direction uncertainty will move the initial extraction, like it was in the case of full monopoly. In our numerical examples with a log-linear demand function we found that the initial extraction was higher in the case of uncertainty than in the case of certainty. This is the opposite result of of what we found with the log-linear demand function in the case of full monopoly.

The effect of risk aversion is the same in the present case as in the case of full monopoly: Whenever risk aversion affects the monopolist's solution, the initial resource extraction will be lower in the case of risk aversion than in the case of risk neutrality.

CHAPTER 9.

CONCLUDING COMMENTS.

9.1. Summary of some important results.

Summaries of the main results are given in the end of each of the earlier chapters. This section will therefore not go through all these results in detail. However, some of our findings are collected in table 9.1. This table shows how the resource extraction in period 1 differs between different situations. In setting up the table, the possibility of corner solutions giving an initial extraction equal to the maximal physical limit is disregarded.

The resource extraction in period 1 under various market structures and how it is affected by various factors.

		I Social Optimum	II Perfect Competition	III Full Monopoly	IV Monopoly only of the Natural Resource
UNCERTAIN SUBSTITUTE	Comparison assuming risk neutrality	I and II equal		usually lower than I	lower than or equal to III, usually lower than I
	Effect of higher π	higher	higher	higher or unaffected	lower, unaffected or higher
	Effect of risk aversion	lower	higher	lower or unaffected	lower, uanffected or higher
UNCERTAIN RESOURCE STOCK	Comparison assuming risk neutrality	I and II equal		usually lower than I	lower than or equal to III, usually lower than I
	Effect of uncertainty assuming risk neutrality	I and II unaffected		lower, unaffected or higher	lower, unaffected or higher
	Effect of risk aversion	I and II unaffected		lower or unaffected	lower or unaffected

Table 9.1

Let us repeat some important conclusions which can be read out of table 9.1. For both types of monopoly, the table states that the initial resource extraction under monopoly usually will be lower than what is socially optimal. More precisely, we have shown that a *sufficient* condition for this to hold is that the demand elasticity is higher the higher the resource price is. In the case of full certainty and no substitute (and zero extraction costs, which we have assumed throughout our analysis) it is easy to see (cf. the analysis in section 4.1, pp. 184-6) that if the demand elasticity declines (is constant) as the price becomes higher, the monopolist will extract more (the same) in the first period that what is socially optimal. This last conclusion no longer holds when a backstop technology will become feasible in period 2 with some positive probability. In particular, when the demand elasticity was constant we found that both monopoly cases would have a lower initial extraction than what was socially optimal as long as the probability of the backstop technology becoming available (=π) was positive. Our numerical examples indicated that when π was high the initial extraction of a monopolist - especially when this monopolist only controlled resource extraction - could be considerably lower than what was optimal. However, as was pointed out in chapter 4, whether or not a large deviation between actual and optimal extraction implied a large welfare loss depends crucially on the demand function, among other factors.

From table 9.1 we see that, in the absence of risk aversion, a monopolist not controlling the backstop technology never will extract more initially than a monopolist controlling both the substitute and the resource. This conclusion - which might seem surprising - is very similar to one of the conclusions in Hoel (1977b). Here the same result was found, except when the initial price in the case of full monopoly exceeded the cost of producing the substitute. The reason why this exception does not apply in the present analysis is that we have assumed throughout the analysis that no backstop technology is available in the first period.

When the availability of the backstop technology is uncertain, and competitive resource extraction firms have risk aversion, the competitive solution will give a higher initial resource extraction than what is socially optimal. We have also shown that risk aversion can reverse the relationship discussed above between our two monopoly cases. Furthermore, even when the demand elasticity is a non-decreasing function of the resource price a risk averse monopolist not controlling the backstop technology may have a higher initial extraction than what is socially optimal. In particular, our numerical examples demonstrated that this could occur with linear and log-linear demand functions, unlike in the case of certainty (see Hoel, 1977 a,b).

With the assumptions we have made, risk aversion has no effect on the optimal and competitive resource extrection when it is the size of the resource stock which is uncertain. In this case it ålso follows from table 9.1 that the initial extraction of a monopolist will be lower or equal when the monopolist has risk aversion than when the monopolist is risk neutral. A consequence of the two conclusions above is that for both monopoly cases a sufficient condition for the monopolist's initial extraction to be lower than what is socially optimal is that the demand elasticity is a non-decreasing function of the resource price.

9.2. Optimal resource extraction and market economies.

Several economists and non-economists have claimed that there is a tendency for market economies to exhaust non-renewable natural resources too fast. Hopefully, the present study sheds some light on these topics. As mentioned in the introduction, the sum of all our assumptions makes the analysis rather restrictive. In spite of this, several results have been obtained which at least point out some possible consequences for optimal and market determined resource extraction when uncertainty and risk aversion are introduced. Some of our results concerning the comparison of various market structures with the social optimum are summarized below.

When there is no possibility of a backstop technology becoming available, and the resource stock is known with certainty, the competitive solution will be socially optimal. In this case a monopolist usually will have an initial extraction which is lower than what is optimal. These conclusions hold (and are even strengthened in the case of monopoly) also when a backstop technology is known to be available in the second period. If we in the latter case introduce uncertainty with respect to the size of the resource stock, our conclusions above still hold, and with risk aversion the results concerning the monopoly cases are strengthened.

Compared with the situation with no uncertainty and no backstop technology, the introduction of a backstop technology, uncertainty with respect to the size of the resource stock and risk aversion does not change the result that competition gives an optimal resource extraction, and strengthens the conclusion that a monopolist extracts too little initially. These conclusions remain valid also when the availability of a backstop technology is uncertain, as long as risk aversion is disregarded. However, the introduction of risk aversion in this case changes these results. Competitive risk averse firms will extract more in the first period than what is optimal. It is also possible for excessive extraction to occur in the c of monopoly, if the monopolist has risk aversion and does not control the backstop technology. If society as a whole is risk neutral, however, a risk averse monopolist controlling both the resource and the backstop technology will also in this case usually extract less of the resource initially than what is optimal.

The results above seem to indicate that it is more likely that a market economy extracts too little than too much of a natural resource in the first period. The only case where we find a market economy extracting too much initially is when we have the combination of an uncertain backstop technology, risk aversion and resource extracting firms not controlling the backstop technology. However, this may be an important case in the real world. In particular, if resource extracting firms in most market economies are closer to being competitive than monopolistic, the importance of this tendency to extract more than what is optimal may well be stronger than the tendency for monopolistic firms to extract less than what is optimal.

Throughout our analysis, we have assumed that there is no disagreement between different agents in the economy about the size of the resource stock, the probability of a backstop technology becoming available, etc. This is obviously an unrealistic description of the true world. Let us briefly investigate the consequences of such disagreement, considering only the optimal and competitive solution. The way our model in chapter 6 is formulated, it will make no difference to the conclusions there if competitive firms and society as a whole have different subjective probability distributions concerning the outcomes of the exploration activity. This result does of course not carry over to all other reasonable specifications of our problem. To see this, look at the case where it is not certain that the backstop technology will become available. We have only treated this case assuming that the resource stock was known with certainty. However, disagreement about the true size of the resource stock can be taken care of by assuming that different agents have different expectations about the true size, although each agent holds his expectation with certainty. The optimal and competitive results for this case are given in sections 2.2 and 3.2 (cf. (2.5), (2.6) and (3.13)). From the analysis in these sections it is clear that the larger the resource stock is believed to be, the larger is the initial extraction. In particular, if competitive resource extracting firms are more"technologically optimistic" than society as a whole[1)] (i.e. competitive firms believe that the total resource stock is larger than what society as a whole believes), this will imply that the competitive resource extraction in the first period is higher than what is socially optimal.

A different form of "technological optimism" than the one mentioned above could be that the competitive firms have a larger subjective probability of a backstop technology becoming available ($=\pi$) than society as a whole has. From the same formulas as mentioned above we see that we also in this case would find that the competitive extraction was too high initially.

---

1)"Society as a whole" is a somewhat dubious concept. In the present context it is meant the government, central planning agency or similar, supposed in some sense to represent some average of the various opinions which exist in society.

One type of uncertainty which we have disregarded in the present analysis is various types of political uncertainty. More precisely, this is uncertainty facing privately owned firms who feel that there is a risk of future expropriation, tax increase, price regulation or similar. This type of uncertainty has been analyzed by Heal (1975) and Long (1975), who conclude that the effect of such uncertainty is to increase the initial resource extraction above the socially optimal rate. The analysis in sections 2 and 3 can be used to illustrate the consequence of one type of political uncertainty: Assume that there is no possibility of a backstop technology becoming available, so that the socially optimal resource extraction follows from (2.5) and (2.6) with $\pi = 0$. The competitive resource extracting firms believe there is a probability π that the government will impose a tax or maximal price in period 2 implying that the net resource price facing the firms will be c. In this case the competitive solution will follow from (3.13), with $\pi^* \geqq \pi$ depending on whether or not the firms are risk averse. In other words, this political uncertainty will imply that the competitive firms extract more initially than what is socially optimal. From our numerical examples in sections 2 and 3 it is clear that if the competitive firms are "politically pessimistic" (i.e. have a high π), this bias towards too much resource extraction may be quite large.

From various statements, reports etc. from buisness leaders, one often gets the impression that these leaders are more "technologically optimistic" and more "politically pessimistic" than society as a whole. If this is true also for the resource extracting industry, our reasoning above indicates that this may be an important bias in the direction of market economies having a higher rate of resource extraction than what is socially optimal.

It is obviously impossible to give a general answer to the question of whether or not market economies usually have a higher rate of resource extraction than what is socially optimal. However, this section has mentioned several factors giving a market economy a bias in the direction of overextraction. Even in the presence of a monopolized extracting industry one might therefore well find that a market economy extracts a resource faster than what is socially optimal.

APPENDIX.

In this appendix we wish to prove that the solution to the problem of maximizing (1.11) satisfies the inequality (1.14). To be more precise, our original optimization problem, which we shall call problem P, is as follows:

Problem P:

Maximize $W = \psi(y(\cdot))$

subject to

(A.1) $\dot{K}(t) = \Phi(K(t), x_1(t) + x_2(t), t) - c_1x_1(t) - c_2x_2(t) - y(t)$,

(A.2) $\dot{S}(t) = -x_1(t)$,

(A.3) $K(0) = K_o$, $\quad K(T) \geqq K_T$,

(A.4) $S(0) = S_o$, $\quad S(T) \geqq 0$,

(A.5) $x_i(t) \geqq 0 \qquad i=1,2$,

(A.6) $y(t) \geqq 0$.

The functional $\psi(y(\cdot))$ has the properties mentioned after (1.11) in section 1.3. The relations (A.2) and (A.4) takes care of the constraint on the resource extraction, S(t) stands for the remaining resource deposit at time t.

Denote a solution to this problem by $(\hat{y}(\cdot), \hat{x}_1(\cdot), \hat{x}_2(\cdot), \hat{K}(\cdot), \hat{S}(\cdot))$. Now $(\hat{x}_1(\cdot), \hat{x}_2(\cdot), \hat{K}(\cdot), \hat{S}(\cdot))$ must also be a solution to the following problem (problem P'):

Problem P':

$$\text{Maximize} \quad K(t) = \int_0^T [\Phi(K(t),\ x_1(t)+x_1(t)+x_2(t),t)-c_1x_1(t)-c_2x_2(t)-\hat{y}(t)]dt - K_o$$

subject to

(A.1') $\dot{K}(t) = \Phi(K(t),\ x_1(t)+x_2(t),t) - c_1x_1(t) - c_2x_2(t) - \hat{y}(t)$,

(A.3') $K(0) = K_o$, $\quad K(T)$ free,

as well as (A.2), (A.4) and (A.5).

The reason why the solution to problem P also must be a solution to P' is easy to see: Assume that this is not the case, i.e. that some solution $\tilde{x}_1(\cdot), \tilde{x}_2(\cdot), \tilde{K}(\cdot), \tilde{S}(\cdot)$ gives $\tilde{K}(T) > \hat{K}(T)$. In this case one could have increased $\hat{y}(t)$ for t near to T by reducing $\dot{K}(t)$ near T compared with the investment necessary to give $K(T) = \hat{K}(T)$. This would be allowed in problem P because $\tilde{K}(T) > \hat{K}(T) \geqq K_T$. But such a possibility of increasing $\hat{y}(t)$ means that $(\hat{y}(\cdot), \hat{x}_1(\cdot), \hat{x}_2(\cdot), \hat{K}(\cdot), \hat{S}(\cdot))$ cannot be a solution to problem P. This contradiction proves that the solution to problem P also must be a solution to problem P'.

The Hamiltonian corresponding to problem P' is

(A.7) $$H(K,S,x_1,x_2,\gamma,\lambda,t) = (1+\gamma)[\Phi(K,x_1+x_2,t)-c_1x_1-c_2x_2-\hat{y}(t)] - \lambda x_1.$$ [1)]

---

1) We have set the auxiliary variable belonging to the intergrand in K(t) equal to one without proving that it cannot be zero. This proof, however, is straightforward.

The necessary conditions which our solution must satisfy are (see for instance Seierstad and Sydsæter, 1977, pp. 368-70):

(A.8) $\dot{\gamma}(t) = -(1+\gamma(t))r(t)$

where

(A.9) $r(t) = \dfrac{\partial\Phi(\hat{K}(t),\ \hat{x}_1(t)+\hat{x}_2(t),\ t)}{\partial K}$,

(A.10) $\dot{\lambda}(t) = 0,$

(A.11) $\gamma(T) = 0$, $\lambda(T) \geqq 0,$

and finally

(A.12) $(1+\gamma(t))[\Phi(\hat{K}(t),\hat{x}_1(t)+\hat{x}_2(t),t)-c_1\hat{x}_1(t)-c_2\hat{x}_2(t)] - \lambda(t)\hat{x}_1(t)$

$\geqq (1+\gamma(t))[\Phi(\hat{K}(t),x_1(t)+x_2(t),t)-c_1x_1(t)-c_2x_2(t)] - \lambda(t)x_1(t)$

for all $x_1(t)$ and $x_2(t)$ satisfying (A.5).

From (A.8) we see that

$$1+\gamma(t) = (1+\gamma(0))e^{-\int_0^t r(\tau)d\tau} .$$

Inserting this into (A.12) and defining

$$\lambda' = \frac{\lambda(t)}{1+\gamma(0)} ,$$

which is constant and non-negative because of (A.9) and (A.11), gives us

$$(A.13)\qquad e^{-\int_0^t r(\tau)d\tau}[\Phi(\hat{K}(t),\hat{x}_1(t)+\hat{x}_2(t),t)-c_1\hat{x}_1(t)-c_2\hat{x}_2(t)] - \lambda'\hat{x}_1(t)$$

$$\geqq e^{-\int_0^t r(\tau)d\tau}[\Phi(\hat{K}(t),x_1(t)+x_2(t),t)-c_1x_1(t)-c_2x_2(t)] - \lambda'x_1(t).$$

So far, we have shown that the solution to problem P must satisfy (A.13) where λ' is some non-negative number. The last step in our proof is to show that this implies that the inequality given by (1.14) must hold. The inequality given by (1.14) states that $(\hat{x}_1(\cdot),\hat{x}_2(\cdot),\hat{S}(\cdot))$ must be a solution to the following problem (problem P''):

Problem P'':

Maximize $$J = \int_0^T e^{-\int_0^t r(\tau)d\tau}[\Phi(\hat{K}(t),x_1(t)+x_2(t),t)-c_1x_1(t)-c_2x_2(t)]dt$$

subject to (A.2), (A.4) and (A.5).

A *sufficient* condition for $(\hat{x}_1(\cdot),\hat{x}_2(\cdot),\hat{S}(\cdot))$ to be a solution to this problem is that we can find a continuous function $\mu(t)$ such that[1)]

$$(A.14)\qquad \dot{\mu}(t) = -\frac{\partial H''(\hat{S}(t),\hat{x}_1(t),\hat{x}_2(t),\mu(t),t}{\partial S}$$

1) See Seierstad and Sydsæter (1977, pp. 368-70).

where

$$\text{(A.15)}\qquad H''(S,x_1,x_2,\mu,t) = e^{-\int_0^t r(\tau)d\tau}\,[\Phi(K_1x_1+x_1t)-c_1x_1-c_2x_2] - \mu x_1,$$

$$\text{(A.16)}\qquad \mu(T) \geqq 0,$$

and finally,

$$\text{(A.17)}\qquad H''(\hat{S}(t),\hat{x}_1(t),\hat{x}_2(t),\mu(t),t) \geqq H''(\hat{S}(t),x_1(t),x_2(t),\mu(t),t)$$

for all $x_1(t)$ and $x_2(t)$ satisfying (A.5).

From (A.14) and (A.15) we see that $\mu(t)$ must be constant. Together with (A.17) and (A.15), this means we are trying to find a constant μ satisfying

$$\text{(A.18)}\qquad e^{-\int_0^t r(\tau)d\tau}\,[\Phi(\hat{K}(t),\hat{x}_1(t)+\hat{x}_2(t),t)-c_1\hat{x}_1(t)-c_2\hat{x}_2(t)] - \mu\hat{x}_1(t)$$

$$\geqq e^{-\int_0^t r(\tau)d\tau}\,[\Phi(\hat{K}(t),x_1(t)+x_2(t),t)-c_1x_1(t)-c_2x_2(t)] - \mu x_1(t)$$

But for $\mu=\lambda'$ this inequality is identical to (A.13). Our sufficiency condition therefore holds when $\mu=\lambda'$, i.e. we have proved that the solution to problem P also is a solution to problem P''. Or in other words, we have proved that the solution to problem P must satisfy the inequality given by (1.14).

References:

Arrow, K.J. (1965), *Aspects of the Theory of Risk-Bearing*, The Academic Book Store, Helsinki.

Cropper, M.L. (1976), "Regulating Actitivities with Catastrophic Environmental Effects", *Journal of Environmental Economics and Management*, 3 (1, June), pp. 1-15.

Dasgupta, P. and Heal, G.M. (1974), "The Optimal Depletion of Exhaustible Resources, *Review of Economic Studies, Symposium on the Economics of Exhaustible Resources*, pp. 3-28.

Dasgupta, P. and Stiglitz, J .E. (1976), "Uncertainty and the Rate of Extraction under Alternative Institutional Arrangements", Technical Report No. 179 from Institute for Mathematical Studies in the Social Sciences, Stanford University, Stanford, California.

Dorfman, R., Samuelson, P. and Solow, R. (1958), *Linear Programming and Economic Analysis*, McGraw-Hill, New York.

Gilbert, R.J. (1976), "Search Strategies for Nonrenewable Resource Deposits", Technical Report No. 196 from Institute for Mathematical Studies in the Social Sciences, Stanford University, Stanford, California.

Gilbert, R.J. (1977), "Resource Extraction with Differential Information", *American Economic Review, Papers and Proceedings*, 67 (4, February), pp. 250-254.

Gilbert, R.J. (1979), "Optimal Depletion of an Uncertain Stock", *Review of Economic Studies*, 46 (1, February), pp. 47-57.

Hanson, D. (1977), "The Allocation of a Natural Resource when the Cost of a Substitute is Uncertain", *Annals of Economic and Social Measurement* 6(2), pp. 189-201.

Heal, G.M. (1975), "Economic Aspects of Natural Resource Depletion", in Pearce, D.W. and Rose, J. (eds.) (1975), *The Economics of Natural Resource Depletion*, Macmillan Press, London, pp. 118-139.

Hoel, M. (1978a), *Resource Extraction under Some Alternative Market Structures*, Mathematical Systems in Economics 39, Verlag Anton Hain, Meisenheim am Glan.

Hoel, M. (1978b), "Resource Extraction, Substitute Production and Monopoly", *Journal of Economic Theory*, 19 (1, October), pp. 28-37.

Hoel, M. (1978c), "Resource Extraction when a Future Substitute has an Uncertain Cost", *Review of Economic Studies*, 45 (3, October), pp. 637-644.

Hotelling, H. (1931), "The Economics of Exhaustible Resources", *Journal of Political Economy*, 39 (2, April), pp. 137-175.

Kay, J. and Mirrlees, J. (1975), "The Desirability of Natural Resource Depletion", in Pearce, D.W. and Rose, J. (eds.) (1975), *The Economics of Natural Resource Depletion*, Macmillan Press, London, pp. 140-176.

Kemp, M. (1976), *Three Topics in the Theory of International Trade*, North-Holland, Amsterdam.

Leland, H. (1972), "Theory of the Firm Facing Uncertain Demand", *American Economic Review*, Vol. 62 (3, June), pp. 278-291.

Lewis, T.R. (1976), "Monopoly Exploitation of an Exhaustible Resource", *Journal of Environmental Economics and Management*, 3 (3, October), pp. 198-204.

Lewis, T.R. (1977), "Attitudes towards Risk and the Optimal Exploitation of an Exhaustible Resource", *Journal of Environmental Economics and Management*, 4 (2, June), pp. 111-119.

Loury, G. (1976), "The Optimum Exploitation of an Unknown Reserve", Discussion Paper No. 225, Center for Mathematical Studies in Economics and Management Science, Northwestern University, Evanston, Illinois.

Long, N.V. (1975). "Resource Extraction under the Uncertainty about Possible Nationalization", *Journal of Economic Theory*, 10 (1, February), pp. 42-53.

Manne, A.S. (1974), "Waiting for the Breeder", *Review of Economic Studies, Symposium on the Economics of Exhaustible Resources*, pp. 47-65.

Massé, P. (1962), *Optimal Investment Decisions*, Prentice-Hall, Englewood, N.J.

von Neumann, J. and Morgenstern, O. (1947), *Theory of Games and Economic Behaviour* (second edition), Princeton University Press, Princeton, N.J.

Nordhaus, W.D. (1973), "The Allocation of Energy Resources", *Brookings Papers on Economic Activity*, No. 3, pp. 529-576.

Pollak, R.A. (1968), "Consistent Planning", *Review of Economic Studies*, 35 (2, April), pp. 201-208.

Pratt, J.W. (1964), "Risk Aversion in the Small and in the Large", *Econometrica*, 32 (1-2, January - April), pp. 122-136.

Sandmo, A. (1971), "On the Theory of the Competitive Firm under Price Uncertainty", *American Economic Review*, 61 (1, March), pp.65-73.

Seierstad, A. and Sydsæter, K. (1977), "Sufficient Conditions in Optimal Control Theory", *International Economic Review*, 18 (2, June), pp. 367-391.

Solow, R.M. (1977), "Monopoly, Uncertainty and Exploration", in A.S. Blinder & P. Friedman (eds.): *Natural Resources, Uncertainty, and General Equilibrium Systems: Essays in Memory of Rafael Lusky*, Academic Press, New York.

Stiglitz, J.E. (1976), "Monopoly and the Rate of Extraction of Exhaustible Resources", *American Economic Review,* 66 (4, September), pp. 655-661.

Strotz, R.H. (1955), "Myopia and Inconsistency in Dynamic Utility Maximization", *Review of Economic Studies,* 23 (3), pp. 165-180.

Sweeney, J.L. (1977), "Economics of Depletable Resources: Market Forces and Intertemporal Bias", *Review of Economic Studies* 44 (1, February), pp. 125-142.

Weinstein, M.C. and Zeckhauser, R.J. (1974), "Use Patterns for Depletable and Recycleable Resources", *Review of Economic Studies, Symposium on the Economics of Exhaustible Resources,* pp. 67-88.

Weinstein, M.C. and Zeckhauser, R.J. (1975), "The Optimal Consumption of Depletable Natural Resources", *Quarterly Journal of Economics,* 89 (3, August), pp. 371-392.